Poems by Kolki

Absolutely Humane

© Copyright 2007 Deepak Sarkar.
All rights reserved. No part of this publication may be reproduced, stored in a retrieval system, or transmitted, in any form or by any means, electronic, mechanical, photocopying, recording, or otherwise, without the written prior permission of the author.

Note for Librarians: A cataloguing record for this book is available from Library and Archives Canada at www.collectionscanada.ca/amicus/index-e.html
ISBN 978-1-4251-2395-6

Printed in Victoria, BC, Canada. Printed on paper with minimum 30% recycled fibre.
Trafford's print shop runs on "green energy" from solar, wind and other environmentally-friendly power sources.

Offices in Canada, USA, Ireland and UK

10 9 8 7 6 5 4 3 2 1

Dedicated to my wonderful wife, family, friends and the lovebirds…..

Table of Contents

Poem	Page
Diplomacy	8
Song of Equity	9
Eternal	10
Transit	11
Universal God	12
Utopia	13
War Crimes	14
A Day of Non-Violence	15
Day of Thinking	16
True Friend	17
Inspiration	18
Allies	19
Teacher	20
What is Love?	21
Democracy	22
Hijack	23
Evil Thought	25
Better World	27
Once Upon a Time	28
Rich	30
Patriot	31
Peace Activist	32
Villains	33
Illusion	34
Magic	35
Lies	36
Truth	37
Pro	38
Covenant	39
Pre-Emptive Strikes	40
War of Terror	41
Remote Control Terror	42
Pilot's Nightmare	43
Guantanamo Bay	45

Table of Contents (Cont.)

Poem	**Page**
Felons	47
Miracle	48
Silent God	50
Not Enslaved	51
Another	52
So What?	54
Devotion	55
Offerings	56
Canadian Pride	57
Canadian	58
American Pride	59
Proud Citizen	61
Pro-American	62
Smart	63
Good Neighbour	64
Violence	65
Killings	67
Lost Sound	68
Baptism–Initiation	69
Faith	70
Spring	71
Window	72
Father's Day	73
Son	74
Loneliness	75
Happiness	76
Pain	77
Worth	78
Nightmares	79
Coffee	80
In Vain	81
Vegetarian World	82
Spirit of Victoria	84
What is New Year	85

Table of Contents (Cont.)

Poem	Page
Universal Celebration	86
Fallen Leaves	87
Mamma Didn't Know	88
Angels	89
Marie	90
Jingle Bell (New)	91
Eid ul-Fitr	92
Vegetarian	93
Illegal Immigrants (Aliens)	94
Co-existence	96
Bunny	97
Earth	98
Natural Rhythm	99
Trinity	101
Radha	102
Electromagnetics	103
Churning	105
OM	106
Mantra-Yagna	107
Conservative	109
Fallen Soldiers	111
Journalists	112
Dying	113
Peace	114
Life Is Simple	115
Stock Market	116
Tax	117
God	118
From Jesus' Dairy	119
Wish List	122
NATO	124
OIL	126
National Security	127

Table of Contents (Cont.)

Poem	Page
Birth Control Pills	128
Another Day	129
Just Being Black	130
Free Market Oil	132
Thanks	133
Unity through Celebration	134
Without A President	135
Health	136
Snacks	137
Healthcare	138
Homeless	140
Peace Now	141
H1B VISA	142
Village Path	144
New Born	145
Anniversary	146
Age Two	147
Happy Birthday	148
Cafeteria	149
Beauty	150
Dream	151
Expectation	152
Stranger	153
Flying	154
Free	155
Love	157
Hesitation	158
Confession	159
Jackpot	160
Darkness	161
Hope	162
Original	163
Beautiful	164
Therapy	165

Table of Contents (Cont.)

Poem	Page
Winner	166
Imagination	167
Dilemma	168
Deceiving	169
Forget	170
Diwali – The Festival of Light	171
Halloween	172
Cry	173
Waiting for You	174
Recovery	175
Real Love	176
Irreversible	179
Funeral	180
Rejuvenate	182
Return	183
Saying of Kolki	184
War-Like	193
New Pearl Harbour	194
9/11 Hijacking	196
Daniel Pearl	198
Inconvenient Truth	200
Without 9/11	203
Terrorism	204
Delegation	206
Expression	207
21st Century Stake	208
Pests	210
Homey	211
Heir	212
Mean	213
Dead End	214
Renounce	215
Palestine	216

Table of Contents (Cont.)

Poem	**Page**
Silent Cry	217
Betrayal	218
How Can We Help?	219
Recycling	220
Super Power	221
Universal Super Power	222
Participatory Democracy	223
Democratic Security	226
Intelligence	227
American Orange Revolution	228
Apology	230
Santa Claus	231
Got You	233
Thank You	234
Death	235
About Kolki	236

References: All Highlights and Underlines in this book are internet links for appropriate related or supporting material for epic poems and poems revealing truth in a poetic way. All interested readers are requested to visit the online poetry site www.kolki.com to explore the fact finding mission.

Diplomacy
(Dedicated to World wide Peace)

Let love, mercy and mutual understanding
Be the tools for world diplomacy!
Bridging all the gaps and barriers
Created by military dominance and supremacy!

A pen is mightier than a sword!
Let us prove once more!
A mind above doubts and fear -
Can break the ice, 'status quo', forever!

A heart which eager to love
Can win enemy as friends!
The ears which are ready to listen
Ignore all strategic military intelligence!

When arms are ready to embrace
Thoughts are energised in optimism!
All human problems find solution
In honestly brokered communication!

Song of Equity
(Dedicated to world peace and harmony, written: 12/08/2005)

Come let us hold our hands
Come let us sing along
The joyous tune together
Let the waves ring and ring in the air
As they traverse to the horizon
Unleashing unspoken protests and grievances
Bringing us a new dawn!

Come let us love each other
Fill our hearts with loving thoughts
Ending all distant separation -
Of blind judgement and superstition
Deep seeded in age-old darkness!
Transforming doubts of fear to kindness
Bathing in light of conscious-river
Be enlightened humble and richer!

Come let us work together!
Fight for our rights everywhere!
Enjoy all fruits of thoughtful labour
Concealing exploitation in history forever!
Embracing differences for a grand union
Celebrating hope in trust and just freedom!
Believing in trivial humane solutions
For all inherited problems and illusions!

Eternal

(Dedicated to **Friendship Day**, Written at Sayward Hill Golf Club, June 2006, Victoria)

I needed a hug!
You sent wonderful breeze in sudden gust!
I needed warmth!
You rose as the Sun!
I lost all faith!
You showed me the universal light I can bathe!
I needed companion!
You became all beings with loving emotions!
I was hungry!
You offered fruits, grains, nuts, vegetables, milk, and honey!
I felt tired and sleepy!
You laid out bed of grass under trees!
I was without a home!
You gave me the world in your universal abode!
I was craving to feel your presence!
You gave me the vision to see you as omnipresent!
I wanted to express gratitude for everything –
You reminded me your love is unconditional eternal blessings!

Transit

We come and depart
Like the tides in the ocean
The way clouds appear and disappear
Experience sorrows and happiness
Resembling light and darkness!

We try to love
Only to feel half-heartedness!
We try to speak our mind
Words make it meaningless!
We collect things of lust
Only to find them useless!
We find our better half
Only to know half way!
We learn to know it all
Only to feel frustrated!
We cheer having it all
Only to suffer emptiness!
We feel proud of family and friends
At the end embrace loneliness!
But after all bitterness
We most cherish being on this planet!

Universal God
(Dedicated to May Day for an united world)

Universal God gave us a common sun
The rays reach every corner of the world!
One moon pulls oceans bringing tides
Poetic light covers our planet during moonlit night!

Air composed of constituents of such proportional manner
Every animal and plants can breathe happily together!
Water contains elements so balanced in nature
It quenches thirst for every being without stature!

Soil is made of such compassionate supportive matter
Every plant root finds food and shelter in care!
One ground acts as infinite charge reservoir
Accommodate lightening and return for all electric power!

One blood of same texture and colour
Flowing through human veins everywhere!
Rain and snow cover lands with heavenly showers
That touches all in the region without bias!

Animal evolved as human with a brain enlightened
Thanked God almighty for eternal blessings and kindness!
Whenever a God promises our world only to few chosen
That voice must be from a partisan illegal alien!

Utopia
(Dedicated to family values)

Imagine! A day with hope!
The Sun is shining –
Blossom of flowers is everywhere;
Birds are chirping –
Overshadowing the noise of civilization.
Everywhere you look –
Just sign of joy and joy and joy.

A day of re-union!
All family members together
None working late or week-ends,
Without the excuse of illness or guest
Just laughter and laughter and laughter together.

A day of recollection!
Where you were, where you are,
What you wanted to be,
What you have been, just reminiscences......

A day of consciousness!
Whether we are economically better
Whether others suffering to make us fortunate
Whether we have little time for the planet
Whether we became self-centered
Whether some things may have been done differently!
Just re-evaluation.......

A day of peace!
Questioning past justification of wars-
How all or some could have been avoided
Knowing who benefits from a war
Stopping violence everywhere
Just love and love and love!
For everybody and everything around you
Just love and love and love....

War Crimes
(Dedicated to all who suffers the wrath of Supremacy)

Judges punish citizens
For felony, battering and crimes!
Lawyers build cases for the jurors
Proving innocence or guilty as charged!

Nations join together -
To stop imperialism by super power!
Creating United Nations, International Court
With votes, veto and legal power!

But super power can buy votes!
Bribes lawyers or apply own veto for war!
Dividing nations creating allied power
Attack and occupy country at peace
Exercising brutal military power!
Killing, terrifying, abusing civilians
Destroying culture ancient and dear!

International court remains helpless and silent!
As war crime tribunals punish victims of violence!
While criminals of wars celebrate victory
Making world more fragile, divided and angry!

A Day of Non Violence
(Dedicated to Gandhi Day)

Imagine –
A Day in this world –
No cows being slaughtered
No pig or goat or lamb being butchered
No chicken head severed
No fish out of water
No eggs broken –
Just for one day!

A Day –
No wars being fought anywhere
No one being killed or assassinated
No one being raped or abused
No foetus being aborted
No child being circumcised
All Civil Wars take a pause
Just like Mecca of disarming and friendliness!

A Day –
No bird being shot at
No animal being tortured in medical labs
No hunting in the forests
Sound of firearms replaced with sound of nature
No trees being logged
No weapons being tested
No guns or arms being sold
All army or guerrilla training stopped?
Because it's a 'Day of Non Violence'!
A chance to feel within the joy of co-existence!

Day of Thinking
(Dedicated to realization of the fragileness of the Planet Earth)
[Isn't rapid digging, drilling and logging alien mentality?
Aboriginals lived thousands of years co-existing! Let's rethink!
<u>Kolki</u>]

Wouldn't it be nice if we had a Day only to think!
No work, play, party, news, golf, or (Internet) surfing!
No chatting, gossiping, socializing, camping or formal dining!
Everything is closed and everybody at home just vegetating!

No electricity, gas, gasoline, newspaper or mail delivery!
No garbage pick up, lawn mowing, cleaning or pruning!
No mining, oil drilling, logging, hunting, boating or fishing!
No cooking; Just left over, nutty salad, fruits and dairy!

No car, bus or train running; no ships sailing; no airplanes flying!
No speed boating, motor-cycling, fitness or aerobic training!
No television, video game, barbeque or block gathering!
Civilization stops for a day except emergency caring!

Just to be quiet and enjoy the world around -
Leisurely sitting, walking, gardening, meditating!
Listening to the ground!
Letting the brain unwind in quietness void of human made sounds!
To review, re-visit, in mind; happenings around year-round!
Watching and feeling Earth rotates around the Sun!

Some will worry about job and economy!
But nothing will happen except world breaths happily!
If God in Bible needed rest after seven days of creativity -
Mother Earth needs a day at least once a year for healing -
To recover from ongoing day to day civilized hostilities!

True Friend
(Dedicated to universal friendship)

A true friend believes in –
Once a friend means always a friend!
That good times are to relish friendship
And bad times are to test the limit!
That distance merely keep them apart -
Because the feeling is deep inside the heart!

A true friend enjoys your very existence -
Expressing unconditional love and care!
Appreciating inner and physical qualities
Bringing out the very best in you
Enriching your mind and true vision
Through constructive criticism when needed -
Enlightening the path toward freedom!

A true friendship is above all social limitations -
Crossing barriers of superstitions, space and time,
Recognizing the souls bound by cosmic links!
Succeeding severe challenges and storms -
Believing in eternal love, care and forgiveness!
A true friend is a friend indeed -
Always standing by you to respond to a need!

Inspiration

(Dedicated to true worldwide love and friendship)
[Hope Valentine's Day spreads the message of true love and friendship – Kolki]

Friend!
If you ever feel depressed!
Or demoralized from many stress!
Or have doubts on your own self!
Or lose faith in life itself!
Remember that someone somewhere –
Eagerly waiting to be your soulmate!
Wishes to inspire your loving thoughts expressed!
Prays for you during sunrise and sunset!
Cares for you in every heartbeat and breath -
Always wants you to be at your best!
Sees your smile in every flower that blooms!
Relishes your beauty in wonders as they loom!
Hears your voice in bird songs and thunderous booms!
So, my friend, never lose heart being upset!
Rather believe in what is your best!
Help steer your life the way you see the goal -
Displaying your clean, glowing and spontaneous soul!
Winning hearts with free smile, wisdom and vision!

Allies
(Dedicated to a united world coexisting as neighbour)

The moment one tries to make allies
There is latent hint others are enemies!
Suddenly there are needs for strategies!
As the war game starts the race for <u>supremacy</u>!

What makes some allies others enemies
Is an age old divide and rule policy!
Soon citizens sacrifice freedom for secrecy
As few revive <u>global Feudalism</u> with legitimacy!

Allied forces march on to consolidate power!
Training some citizens to <u>kill</u> as soldiers!
Media sing along songs of patriotic fever
Depriving many from serving their own better!

Friends are superior to allies with anomalies!
Help maintain global peace as Non-aligned entities!
Outsourcing runs Government
from outside by industries!
Long term allies run a country from inside –
Buying politicians, media and military as lobbyists!

Teacher
(Dedicated to all good teachers around the world)

Buddha taught me to keep it simple and direct!
Muhammad asked me to preach away from birth place!
Jesus cautioned me from disciples and friends!
Gandhi guided me to stay on the course of non-violence!
All enlightened me with the universal laws of co-existence!

Krishna taught me to work toward goal without expectation!
Chaitanya urged me to document realization beyond devotion!
Tagore gave me the courage to write neglecting criticism!
Leader's mistakes helped me to control hormonal temptations!
Media ensured –
Pro-Israeli Pro-Military are immune to assassination!

Ocean pounded me with the message of persistence!
Wind whispered relaying art of free flowing deliverance!
Mandela taught me campaign for freedom is best from prison cell!
Dr. King inspired that serving is not monopoly of Chosen brain!
Western leader's actions unmasked that Zionism is not Semitism!
History taught me violence against Palestinian is anti-Semitism!

Democracies around proved most not really ruling by the majority!
Paperless voting fraud can elect minority empowering military!
Holocaust survivors can be united against peace for hostility!
NEOCONS virus can fast infect political conservatives!
High-tech media can really indulge people into gossips!

Mother taught me caring is a property of every sentient being!
Father gave me the art of praying through singing!
Neighbour taught me dig enough to pay bills ensuring safe exit!
Travelling revived my worldwide warm fellow feelings!
Birds amazed me how to live minimally with sharing!
Sun empowered me to illuminate all without racism!
Moon echoed how to shower blessings even when sleeping!

What is Love?
(Dedicated to a loving world)

What is love after all about -?
Probably the biggest question of the universe!
Lovers, poets, psychologists, priests, philosophers,
All have ideas, thoughts, and experience to share!
But more they talk analyzing art of love
Insecurity evolves in reassuring fear and doubts!

To one night believers –
It begins in bar ends in bar, apartment or car!
While physical lovers –
Find ecstasy in genital pleasures!

To truth seeker love is a realization –
Broadens vision to see beyond!
Brings new meaning to freedom
Discovering peace in non-violent religion!

When one feels the treasure of love
Smile becomes spontaneous
Soul recognizes souls as universal
Greetings and blessings forget recognition!

Love makes one think global -
Caring for citizens beyond border!
Generates leaders thoughtful and conscious
Dedicates military to peace as patriots
Enlightens vision to see evil only in aggressors!

Democracy
(Dedicated to a true participatory majority ruled free world)

World has been governed by many custodianships!
Aristocracy, Autocracy, Despotism, Democracy!
Dictatorship, Meritocracy, Oligarchy, Plutocracy!
Republic, Islamic republic, Monarchy, Constitutional Monarchy!
Absolute monarchy, Single-party state, Theocracy and Tyranny!

Each worked with its pros and cons and legitimacy!
As divided world tried its best for stability!
But time and technology have brought us to proximity –
Giving us a wonderful chance to live as one community!
Reuniting people of all sects with elections participatory!

But as we talk about participatory democracy -
Its time to end all constitutional monarchy!
Where idle Monarchs have a history of turning fascist!
Silently working from behind for military supremacy!
Uniting kings and dictators –
To re-establish Feudalistic Oligarchy!

Hijack

(Dedicated to a true democratic free world)
[As people strive to regain freedom and <u>democracy</u>, International Republican Institute helps <u>undone</u> them! <u>Kolki</u>]

Evolved humans engaged them in trading -
Since the dawn of civilized cultural beginning!
When trading was a daring passion of sharing -
God's enormous scattered gifts of eventful blessings!

Industrial age began with commercial mining!
Extracting the body of earth that supports beings!
As few discovered resources of endless profit making -
Hijacked trading as commerce of fast digging and logging!

Evolved people, animals, birds, fishes, watched in agony
Their home family community fell to wrath of mining, deforesting!
Shared ideas, exchanges, goodwill, unity of trading -
Gave in to strategy, dominance, wars of economic profiteering!

Soon they needed military to protect resources, land and money -
Once private to all world citizens by birth without hegemony!
Peaceful free City-States became divided into countries -
Encaging citizens within borders and walls of cruelty!

Enriched with money, power, protection of military privacy -
They became the class of supreme rulers as beholders of nobility!
Invented Kingship, Lordship, laws –
That guaranteed sustainable slavery!
Making free world smaller for many to enrich prison industry!

Religion became hijacked –
Rewriting scriptures to support monarchy!
Science gave in to research of destructive supremacy technology!
Reproductive art of intimacy –
Found market of hot selling pornography!
Natural healers succumbed to profit making drug industry!

Hijack (Cont.)

People sacrificed under commandments too long –
embracing miseries -
As modern history mainly documented kings and their victories!
Still worried about job, health, education, pension, security -
They hardly can equate hijacking to anything than air industry!
As nobles engineer high-tech hijacking of world Democracy!

Evil Thought
(Dedicated to better life for people everywhere)

They asked for competition –
Blaming Government as the reason for social deterioration!
Encouraged tax money for private distribution!
Requiring subsequent subsidies and deregulations!
Preaching 'Mantra' life can only be better under privatization!
Making 'Private Limited' 'Virtual Limited' Corporation!
Devised Tax Cuts for growth and economic solution!
Manufactured robots to take people out of equation -
Demeaning human labour not good enough for competition!

As labourers tried to form union for salvation -
They divided them as exempt and non-exempt separation!
Ensuring some labourers worked hard to maintain division -
As decision makers purposely cut benefits and remuneration!
Encouraged workers to work without leave or vacation!
Yearly fight against less became dangerous media attention!

Encouraged empowered ensuring point of no return -
Employees left with options of salary cuts or massive terminations!
While politicians worry about few mining or logging vocations!

With structured knowledge of robbing public tax money -
They campaign for the virtues of private health care delivery!
Benefit of pension protected under private economy!
Knowing well the funds will disappear or shrink immensely -
Proactively lobbying for raising retirement age universally!

Having built vast private empire -
They need military to protect their assets everywhere!
Ensuring no one can rise as threat to their superpower!
Dismantle unity of Kyoto, International Court, UN Charter!
Desperately in need of a new Pearl Harbour!
They flooded media cyberspace with the 'Al' Virus!
Declared unilaterally pre-emptive strikes as War on Terror!

Evil Thought (Cont.)

Disrespecting rule of law, <u>proof of conviction</u>, silencing victims forever!
Using private media, military, militia, audiovisual fear!

Better World
(Dedicated to all who contribute toward a better world)

[Truth automatically generates faith; People lose faith on a society or system or religion whose foundation is on lies. <u>Kolki</u>]

Friends! Its 21st Century, time to wake up!
We must not rest until things are really better!
Truthful education, peaceful employment, open market-bazaar!
Vibrant community, honest government, humane health care!

Stricter gun control, safer neighbourhood, polite security guards!
Friendly police, community prison, politicians we can trust!
Public media, visionary scientists, soldiers against war!
Patriot military, wise intelligence, guarding international Border!

Pristine environment, clear water, recycling garbage-paper -
Lesser logging, woodless housing, harnessing energy in Nature!
Judicious judges, kind court practices, decisive trial lawyers!
Global prosperity is National security without '<u>War of Terror</u>'!

Centuries passed by repeating history over and over!
Dominant victory always claimed lives of brothers and sisters!
Supremacy doctrine blinded us with lies, slavery and fear -
Thank God we have technology to see them near and clear!

Once Upon A Time
(Dedicated to lost old, a symbol of gold)

Once upon a time –
Humans were scattered in open countryside!
Cities were small blended side by side -
Maintaining charm, art, and cultural pride
Everyone enjoyed fresh air and sunshine!

Grandparents knew all about food-health needs
Parents learnt to care for a family big!
Neighbour helped delivering babies without notice
Raising child was community events not expensive worries!

Food was always organic without pesticides!
Everyone was safe not knowing homicide!
News was more than advertisement, felony and crimes!
Everyone new moderation meant healthy life!

Police were peacekeepers without gun
High rise buildings didn't block sun
People confessed to priests and nuns
For sincere corrections without jail terms!

Gasoline, processed snacks, and carbonated drinks
Were not the main economic engine!
Military, health care, prison, porn industry
Were not in perception even as alien mystery!

People used to greet each other way to market
Where they met local farmers displaying baskets
Fresh flowers, produce, grains and animals
Exchanged hands from their loving children!

Fruits and vegetables were sold in dozens or basket
Price didn't weigh inedible stems or branches!
People could eat vegetable skins for nourishment
Fresh fruits without smell of chemical and waxes!

Once Upon A Time (Cont.)

Children used to look beautiful in school uniform
School yard was not meant for display of fashion
Innocence and adolescence enjoyed learning with fun
No one could think ever a student with a gun!

War among countries had laws even scheduled time
Forbidding barbaric attack on civilians at night!

Politicians knew the meaning of speaking under oath
Without competing for lies or holding truth for votes!
Military meant for defending own country
Not to hurt others beyond border for Supremacy!

Patriot meant one's love and respect for the land
Not who sent another beyond border for invasion!
Jesus meant love, neighbourly and friendliness
Not deadly cross a symbol of dominance!

Rich
(Dedicated to an world full of richness of love and trust)

We all want to be rich!
In an economy that survive and succeed on greed!
While a few are born rich
Others struggle to make ends meet!

Politicians raise expectation in campaign promise
But tax cuts and service cuts only help the rich!
Poor keep on buying lottery making someone else rich
While pay checks fall short of paying bills and fees!

Stock market reinforces the status quo divisive
People with money owning most stocks in industries!
University grooms middle income classics
Diplomas and certificates certify low income basis!

Higher class must exploit the lower for prestige
While the lowest can't exploit stay on welfare traffic!
Some small business grow making fortune in profit
Others blame minimum wage too high to stay competitive!

It's certainly worth to strive for being rich
In mind body communion in communal peace!
Whoever has good spouse, friends and kids –
Can only feel the richness of heavenly bliss!

Patriot
(Dedicated to Veteran's Day to end all military aggressions)

Though we come in the world as citizen -
Boundary beyond our control makes us limited!
Assigning a country with a border well guarded -
Making us patriot to protect land inherited!

Soon we learn about Fatherland or Motherland!
Heroes who fought in many heroic stands!
Died like patriots defending our sky and border -
Against all foreign invasions and intruders!

We become adult inspired by '**Us** versus **Them**'!
From sports to jobs to economy to military race!
Competition grows to beat neighbouring state -
Who can build the military to fight for Supremacy the best!

Defence industries survive on profits a war generates!
Hurriedly spreads media rumours-gossips to build case!
Politicians helplessly rally around momentum for election ease!
End up authorizing, supporting, 'Unjust Illegal War' aggressive!

A true patriot can never send another beyond border!
While hiding in the White House, Parliament or Palace shelter!
Knowing well war means killings among brothers and sisters!
Join soldiers proudly to defend country from attackers!

Peace Activist
(Dedicated to all who suffer for peace missions)

One who loves peace,
Works extra time for peace,
Tries to convince others the goodness in peace
Not yet desensitized with personal needs
Feels sufferings inflicted on innocent beings
By an invading army, militia, mercenary or arsonist
Often gets labelled as peace activist!

Authorities almost always treat them as terrorists!
Anti-social elements in media at best or cops list!
Ignoring threats on self, family and friends
Rising above humiliation during discussions and debates!
Challenging notions implanted by society's creed and greed
Seeing beyond parents religious belief
Works alone or join team providing relief
Bringing solace refuge to those in need!
Effortlessly seeking truth and justice!

Busy worrying, helping, writing or protesting
Often forget powerful eyes have been watching
Conspiring remote controlled suicide bombing
Carefully spying on every move and night staying
Writing suicide notes before slaying
At home, in a hotel room; while walking or jogging!
Emergency crew will cover the lifeless body
Few will remember as a great soul and buddy
Others will believe in rumour, news and stories!

Villains
(Dedicated to true Democracy where society only evolves forward)

Though its passion which inspires people to lead and serve
Makes someone renowned for years to come!
Every now and then a few rise to take us back
In the days of feudal lords now legalized!

Spread the message of greed to enrich the rich
Who in turn fund them to ensure people's defeat!
Lacking world vision and caring compassion
They proudly act as villains dividing nations!

Retreat from global treaties toward peaceful grace
Increase military spending to provoke arms race!
Disrespect international court and open justice
Run a democracy with military control secretive!

Treat earth as a chest of resources infinite
Pass bills to log and mine with alien appetite!
Encourage violence for hegemonic adventures
Ignore established economic, social, scientific literatures!

Mire a nation with deficits, debts and hatred
While a few clap and praise as they celebrate!
Outsource government to private fortresses
Terrorize communities imposing new fees for services!

Manipulate media with doctored opinion poll gains
Strengthen grip on power rewarding other villains!
Need wars to make others pay incurred national debt
Evolve backward inflicting irreversible global damage!

Illusion
(Dedicated to <u>true democracy</u>, <u>rule of law</u> and <u>proof of conviction</u>)

[Why world must give all accused chance to speak with assumption of innocence until proven guilty? Lest we live under <u>criminal intelligence</u>, court and military! <u>Kolki</u>]

It is time for another election!
Politicians using public and soft money with discretion!
Media busy with analysis, polls and characterization!
Industry busy lobbying for more privatization!
Trade unions campaigning for workers and institutions!
Voters weighing tax cuts against universal freedom!

Citizens cast ballots on the day of election -
Hoping the vote counts to bring change per intention!
Media brings results home ending all speculation!
Some feel depressed others joyous celebration!

Victory speech follows the losing concession!
Elected leader trembles with passion and excitation!
Promises beyond campaign for patriotic mission!
Setting the stage for all night celebrations!

Night ends beginning new political ambition!
Leader meets members for overall discussions!
Revitalize commitment for proposal implementation!
Security intelligence briefing starts in close session!

Leader tries to side step dampening conversation!
Wonders who they are above electoral jurisdiction!
Talk with so much authority without much emotion!
Disrupt countries priorities making election an illusion!

Magic
(Dedicated to world wide true democracy)

Sometimes democracy works like magic!
Party in power can tally election results to victory!
Judges can stop vote counts making election mockery!
Citizen's welfare takes back sit for Military priority!
Truth becomes powerless conspiracy!
Conspirators run Government with legitimacy!
Mighty power invades foreign countries for democracy!
Installs dictatorships as convenient allies!
Revolution against occupation becomes insurgency!
Protests for democracy are silenced as militancy!

Lies
(Dedicated to all suffering souls during and after wars, written 12/03/2005)

Presidents always lie under oath to justify wars!
During speeches praising heroic efforts
Without explaining the mission under cover
Hiding true intention raising patriotic fever!

Politicians lie or avoid truth afterwards
Thinking its good for economy and the voters!
Making human the only animal of The Creator -
Who enjoy killing own kind as predators!

Citizens kill citizens with license
Sufferers become labelled as insurgents!
Reporters report from a distance!
Daring ones get abducted, beheaded in cyberspace -
Sensitive true media get bombarded, displaced!

Peace lovers cry, walk with candle and incandescence
As bodies, buildings, beings get annihilated!
People pray, some ignore, some rejoice -
As occupiers kidnap, assassinate, activists providing solace!

Pope tries to mediate in vain -
UN efforts get side tracked for convenience!
Evangelists delighted glorifying revenge!
Buddha sighs, Jesus asks for forgiveness -
Mohammed in disbelief! God bewildered helpless!

Truth
(Dedicated to all victims of lies)

I can speak truth openly without thought of humiliation!
Because I don't belong to an institution!
No one paid me to act honest in sophistication!
Certainly not gaining anything for self gratification!
Have no intention to campaign for future election!
Why can express myself before media characterization!
Unconcerned with worries of journalistic speculations!
Not lobbying on behalf of any platform with affiliation
Finally, speech is not my professional transaction!

We are taught to be truthful throughout childhood
But we learn the adjustments reaching adulthood!
Soon get used to diplomacy embedding falsehood
Often knowingly withhold truth for livelihood!
Cautiously avoid inquisitive child throughout parenthood
Nation's intelligence hides truth to save Nationhood
Elected officials forget hands still on the holy book!

When people get used to lying under condition!
An honest and just society only lives in imagination!
Guarding truth is a game in corporate competition!
Military ensures national security –
blacking out documentation!
Celebrities learn to lie looking smart with fashion!
Religious leaders make stories during Evangelic mission!
Truth seekers try in vein to remind implication -
Avoiding truth only leads to eventual self destruction!

Pro
(Dedicated to Pro-Humane world)

It's amazing –
Pro-military, pro-war, pro-Israeli enthusiasm –
Are never shut out physically or by media assassination!
Pro-foetus voices of anti-abortion -
Are equivocally for death sentence, invasion and destruction!
Supporters of pre-emptive strikes –
Fight united against gun control!
Politicians for faith, privacy, against nationalization -
Are always for pollution, tough on crime and militarization!
Instruments of Democratization -
Are against open government – for secret annihilation!
Against Rule of Law and Proof of Conviction!

Covenant
(Dedicated to universal consciousness)

Universal God gave people on earth
Guaranteed sun shine free of charge!
Pristine air, water, soil, rain and clouds!
Trees, birds and animals as companion!
Seasons to feel life year around!

Heavenly God came on earth -
Established rule of Patriarchs!
Gave commandments when to sleep and work!
Rights to own universe in private care!
Established blood covenant with chosen heir!
Erasing history of peace with endless wars!

Pre-Emptive Strikes
(Dedicated to peaceful world resolving conflicts before they arise)

Pre-emptive strikes are hazardous intention
Just based on doubts and speculations!
Bypassing rule of law and court of justice!
Punish and kill innocent victims!

It strikes the slaves, employees, citizens!
Destroy countries communities and villages!
To reinforce chosen's grip on power and the process!
Majority always suffer for minority success!

It is the buzzword of the media of military might!
Proof of conviction just another obligation set aside!
But pre-emptive heart begets constructive mind!
Strikes at the cause of sufferings in sight!

Pre-emptive talks can resolve conflicts before they rise!
Renewing contracts before lockouts and strikes!
Handling disputes local or global alike!
Caring for each other sharing burden of life!
Without military genocide of human rights!

War of Terror
(Dedicated to Dr. Martin Luther King, written 1/15/2006)

From Jesus to Gandhi
President Kennedy to Dr. Martin Luther King
Malcolm X to Robert Kennedy
John Lennon to Swedish Prime Minister Olof Palme
Prime Minister Indira Gandhi to Yitzhak Rabin
Whoever dared to ask others to embrace for peace
Were assassinated using well guarded State accomplice
By few powerful minds born Imperialist
Hiding behind National Interests and secrecies
Framing mental patients or bystanders without motive!

Unnoticed unpunished they grow hungry for power
Build private military to fight global drug-war
Ensuring supremacy scripted in prophecy
Act as bloody Messiah invent 'War on Terror'!
Plan, execute, and glorify 'Shock & Awe'
Rapid killings and destruction without law
Blaming fundamentalists, poverty and poor
For all enacted military high-tech horror!

Poverty only teaches people to rise above terror
They face everyday in silence hiding tears!
Pain of sufferings, feeling of hunger
Only encourages one to be free forever.

Terror is the game of military power!
Killing civilians and patriots beyond border
Calling them campaign for Holy Wars
But to victims they are always 'War of Terror'!

Remote Control Terror
(Dedicated to all victims of terror for World Supremacy)

Second World War ended with a sigh of relief
Costing world fifty five million lives we cherish!
Polluting countries filled with debris, mines and shells
Displaying horror of first live nuclear tests!

People gathered, Statesmen met, to make world safe!
They formed UN, signed treaties and hoped for the best!
Ensured dialogs and goodwill prevail -
To end all super power military race!

But from the dead and debris arose another race
Rapidly accumulated power replacing vacant base!
Occupying countries, dividing people without rest
Acting as new guardian with a democratic face!

Blessed with knowledge of atomic weapons -
Soon they invent hydrogen, neutron, cluster, bombs!
Phosphorus, Daisy Cutter, Bunker busters of thousands tons
Actively seeking earth penetrating nuclear bombs!

Succeeded eliminating human with emotions -
Executing missions flying drones by remote control!
Making sorties, sending missiles, gathering intelligence
Even terrorized a comet without global license!

Global Hawks routinely violate most international airspace
Controlled from military Air force Base!
Knowledge acquired from unmanned missions in space
Now being used on earth to erase human race!

From contract killings to detonating nuclear threats
Hijacking passenger flights or luxury Learjet!
Suicide bombings, simulated Tsunami and Earthquakes
World is at the mercy of few human brains!
Possessing remote control technology at its best!

Poems by Kolki About universal well being, peace and love *Absolutely Humane*

Pilot's <u>Nightmare</u>
(Dedicated to ill fated <u>pilots, crew, passengers</u> and victims of 9/11)

Aviation Pilots are always aware -
Of danger behind all commercial hype and fare wars!
That not only they are flying expensive Air Jets
People inside entrusted them with their living faith!

So they train themselves in routes with delicate manoeuvres!
Check everything time and again before flight starts!
Confirm crew at the gate identified valued passengers
Baggage, luggage, customs check all stamped on boarding cards!
Perform tests, final validation as taxiing for take off
Ensure working <u>transponders</u>, hijacking buttons all over!

Soon they go into the air severing ties with full thrust!
Reach altitude wishing everyone a wonderful time in flight!
Cut few jokes with known voice of Air Traffic Controller
Wait for instructions to glide toward destination with cheers!

Suddenly they hear a cockpit voice out of nowhere!
As if ghost flying the plane <u>locking on the transponder</u>!
Even Manual Control doesn't work signalling grave danger!
Desperately <u>try in vain</u> to inform all Ground Receivers!

Recognize the plane is beyond cockpit control
Someone somewhere in charge from ground flying <u>remote control</u>!
Making turns, changing altitudes, re-programming destination path
Endangering other flights, violating passenger safety concerns!

Confused, without Captain's voice and movements irregular
Crew and passenger feel <u>hijacked</u> trembling in fear!
Fanatically press Hijack buttons from all over!
While puzzled not seeing hijackers at all in front or rear!

Soon they see houses, trees, fields as if landing -
Praying and hoping Captain returning for minor technicalities!
Familiar buildings, streets, cars of downtown metropolis!

Pilot's <u>Nightmare</u> (Cont.)

Unaware of real danger smile smelling sigh of relief!

Helpless Captain still pressing buttons for SOS on all frequencies
Screaming, shouting 'Jesus', 'O God' need help its emergency!
As the JET flies straight into a Tower turning into debris!
Ending nightmare which no one survived to tell stories!

Poems by Kolki   About universal well being, peace and love   *Absolutely Humane*

Guantanamo Bay
(Dedicated to all victims who have been silenced depriving them from <u>Rule of Law</u> and <u>Proof of Conviction</u>)

[Ever wonder why Al-Qaeda suspects aren't allowed to speak for themselves before States build their cases? Let's not forget the first question in Democracy – 'What if they are not militant'? We must not live under criminal military and intelligence hiding under National Security and secrecy! <u>Kolki</u>]

Welcome to Guantanamo Bay Cuba!
We specialize in converting innocent people to Al-Qaeda!
<u>Headquartered</u> in the Indian Ocean, Island of <u>Diego Garcia</u>!
The <u>management brain</u> is in Washington DC/Virginia!
Our main North American branch is in <u>Indiana</u>,
Branch offices recruiting all over including <u>Britain</u> and <u>Australia</u>!
Middle Eastern branches are in Kuwait and Saudi Arabia!
The newest branch is in <u>Mississauga</u>, Ontario, Canada!

If you cooperate we will make an offer you can't refuse!
If you don't, you are in for endless torture and abuse!
We make sure no one can hear you but everyone only hears us!
So whatever we tell media is the final words!

We trained for years, detained Palestinians as suicide bombers!
<u>Methodology</u> starts by putting you in solitary cell lighted 24 hours!
Ensuring sleep deprivation waking you up every half an hour!
Interrogations and tortures follow until you surrender –
And prepared to say what we want you to say and follow orders!

You will be chained in hands and legs, looking at the floor all day!
Yet have to finish your meal within five minutes permitted!
Natures call will be rationed prohibited if you ever protest!
You won't be allowed to talk to anyone not even yourself!
No religious practice or bowing to anybody except ourselves!
Until you are baptized as Al-Qaeda wholly committed!

We will train you in all sophisticated bombs and weapons!
You will learn to behead forgetting all superstition!

Guantanamo Bay (Cont.)

How to bring a tower down by creative demolition!
When you pass <u>flight termination</u>, we will send you for mission -
Using private <u>charter flights</u> flying toward worldwide destinations!
Based on demands from allies or to silence countries in opposition!

Occasionally you will be part of a unique secret mission!
As programmable deep water divers inside ocean faults!
<u>Stimulating</u> Earthquakes and Tsunami detonating Neutron Bombs!

People think we only <u>transfer prisoners</u> for <u>outsourcing</u> torture!
Our intelligent media keep the gossip alive with Islamic Posture!
You will be part of our valued team of <u>900,000 plus</u> soldiers -
Running worldwide shadow Governments without UN backlash!
Our political wing keeps politics groovy –
with 'tough on crime' and 'tax cuts'!
Our <u>voting machines</u> are paperless sensitive to remote touch!
World Health Organization resonates with our pandemic cause!
But all these goodness come with only one minor catch!
We will use your video in media for Al-Qaeda broadcast!

Felons
(Dedicated to truth and equal justice for all)

We punish <u>felons</u> for the sake of the communities!
Keeping them isolated in prisons and correctional facilities!
Sometimes killing them in pre-emptive defensive shootings!
Often terminating lives with regrettable death penalty verdicts!

But what happens when felon leaders are free running countries?
Taking fifth, avoiding subpoenas, and withholding proof –
under national securities!
Still visiting foreign lands with dignity pursuing ideology!
Insulting constitutions, honest minds, and the virtues of justice!
Acting as the commander in chief demoralizing soldier's spirits!
Endangering citizens, world and the dreams of truthful society!
Destroying the very fabric of equality under <u>participatory democracy</u>!

Miracle
(Dedicated to day to day Miracles that make life worthwhile)

[Imagine if Pope's Miracle could really resurrect any of the 655,000+ Iraqi's killed by Allied invasion, making him a real Saint! Kolki]

A Pope must show a miracle for <u>beatification</u>!
To be resurrected in Sainthood, above <u>Venerable</u>!
When His Holiness marvels two or more -
Convincing Nuns, Priests, Doctors and Board -
Vatican raises Him to Saint – '<u>Canonization</u>'
Singing all glory to Priestly Miracles!

Biblical prophecies even go furthermore -
With standards for Messiah at home and abroad!
Precisely prescribed as witnessed by millions -
A magical touch must give blinds instant vision!
Cure lame, dumb, leper; bring dead back to mission!
Produce food out of a fish, piece of bread left over -
Feed millions of followers and hungry believers!

Genesis tells them all in scriptures!
All mighty God's miraculous wonders!
Creating Heaven and Earth in seven worldly days -
Resting on eighth day, making it Sabbath Day!
Spreading breads form the sky to feed a New Race!
Killing babies in houses not marked with bloody red!
Using Biological Weapons to create plagues!
Guarding Chosen carefully from human race!

Why search miracles in prophecies and religions?
Ignoring millions happening around!
As the day starts and end in darkness -
Watching our sun reappears, moon rises!
Eternally never breaking promises!
Spinning and moving in speeds at distances -
Without visible links but still connected!

Miracle (Cont.)

Ocean rises, rivers get flooded!
Flowers bloom, grain ripens!
Seeds germinate, plant flourishes!
Animals evolve in Godly manifest!

Birds make trips to distant pilgrimages!
Doctors cure deadly diseases!
Firemen rescue souls from ashes!
Politicians pass bills for the masses!
Scientists bring miracles to houses!
Artists document them as music and verses!

Prophets see them all without glasses!
Convey to people God's miraculous messages!
Spreading through everything as loving touches!
May not be in books, scriptures or in holy scratches!

Poems by Kolki About universal well being, peace and love *Absolutely Humane*

Silent God
(Dedicated to global peace ignoring all divisive politics)
[Honourable Pope Benedict XVI asked himself during his visit to Poland 'Why God was silent?']

Dear Pope! God is never silent!
The message of love is eternal omnipresent!
Many feel it, some hear it, most ignore while a few block it!

God is never silent why Jesus heard it, Muhammad received it!
Buddha realized it, Ashoka preached it!
Why people around the world cry for peace as activists!
Gospels of love spread around the world in lightning speed!
Citizens feel for the left ones as merely a product of greed!
Leaders meet, communicate, to end wars for peace!
Politicians gain courage to rise above media critic
Silent marchers light candles for the dead and buried!

But a few still see victory sign in the cross as Conquerors!
Reviving Constantine's Baptism as holy crusaders!
Using tax money, private media, public trust and power!
Manage to bury the voice under missiles, bombs and terror!
Justify massacres, rapes, abuses, destruction as world guardian!
As the victims wonder how they could do it as Christians!

You hold the key to reveal Jesus' true message -
Exposing power of love concealed in Vatican's Iron chest!
Helping all Christians, Orthodox or Catholic, be united!
Bringing back the gospels alive from Jesus of Nazareth!

Islam regards Jesus as their true prophet!
Hindus always respect Messiah as Lord Vishnu incarnated!
Buddhist loves him as their Bodhisattva in Tibet!
Truth is the ultimate weapon for peace in worldly heaven!
You alone can resurrect holy Jesus loud and clear
Ending all holy crusades bringing friendly cheers -
Reminding Jesus loving Christians –
'BLESSED ARE THE PEACEMAKERS'.!

Not-enslaved

When I was abandoned -
At the height of my life without option
I was bewildered, sad and scared to death!

Tried very hard to go back to life as usual
Pretending everything could be normal
Only to be hurt again hardest
Making me abandoned and wounded!

Faith in God helped me gather strength!
Love in God brought my smile again!
Soon I learned to embrace loneliness -
Without being afraid of myself!

Cooking my own gave the first sense of freedom!
Gardening became fun and leisure at home
Birds, plants, animals became family without chores!

Walking in the woods alone in silence
Gave me a chance to find my inner self!
Listening to the birds the way I never heard before!
Watching rain and storm bringing message of hope!
Feeling of God arose inside free from Scripture's Scrolls!
Always wondered how to have own haircuts!
How one gets massage without a trip to parlor!
Yoga taught me the way of self-massaging
While people wondered about my creative hairstyling!
Lack of medical check ups and testing
Couldn't make me worrying anymore for disease!
My dentist wasn't very happy -
Knowing I learned to clean my own teeth, finally!

Another
(Dedicated to universal consciousness)
[It is always worth being nice to fellow beings at home or afar because we may not have a chance to serve later! <u>Kolki</u>]

Another morning fresh start!
Usual breakfast, lunch, snacks, dinner!
Cleaning with tooth brush and shower!
Pride in makeup, dress up, possession and career!

Another drive or ride through traffic lights!
Rushing to meeting at nine or keep schedule in time!
Cursing at toll booth, freeway jam, cancelled flight!
Another sigh of relief, thanking God, gain is in sight!

Another notice for Christmas or Festive lunch!
Lesser bonus-benefit for downsizing-outsourcing scam!
Quarrel during promotion or contract renewal!
Gift for Birthday, Graduation, Anniversary, Farewell or Reward!

Another death in family, colleague or neighbour!
Old-age sufferings in home or hospital!
Car jacking, accident, police chase fatal!
Drive by shooting hurt unknown dreams shattered!

Another urge to buy lottery!
Wondering how few people get so lucky!
What makes some billionaires very quickly!
How Stock market, Funds, grow while most lose money!

Another election, chance to make things better!
Hijacked by media polling, speculations, fuelled by Defense contracts!
Another rally for green and peace effort!
Sidetracked by analysts spreading biased economic fear!

Another check up with family physician!
Worry about cholesterol, hormone and blood sugar -
Gum disease, toothache, new lens for eye sight!

Another (Cont.)

Test for heart, prostrate or menopausal; remind body aging fragile!
Brain confused, surface diffused but mind still alive!

Another new car, new furniture!
Another uneasy move to new home by peer pressure!
Another war with lies of war-on-terror!
Another Holocaust, war crimes, unpunished closed chapter!

Another laughter, sharing drinks, together!
Trip to health resort or monastery to feel better!
Siren from ambulance, police and fire truck!
This time they are carrying me on stretcher!

So What?
(Dedicated to the virtues of plain living)

So what?
No one treated you like celebrity
Recognised as politician
Scientist or physician
Justice or Lawyer
Corporate Leader or Chief Executive Officer
World renowned game player
Millionaire, billionaire, or stock broker -
Oscar winner, famous composer or photographer?
....

If you had a cozy bed with good neighbour
Enjoyed home made food served at dinner
Thoughtful spouse as companion throughout the year
Children and pets playing in the yard
Bathed in sunshine, embraced moonlit romance
Played lively games for innocent fun
Stared at the blue sky tracking flying kites
Gazed stars at night clear and bright
Walked along beach watching wave's flight!
...
You had wonderful life without much fight!
Without scars of complications or reasons to hide!

Devotion
(Dedicated to all 9/11 related victims of World-Supremacy)

One can memorize all scriptures
Feel proud knowing all about religion!
But no knowledge can replace -
The feeling of devotion!

One can read all about love
Relish all books of romances!
But to feel what love is all about
One has to be in love cherishing emptiness!

Love brings color in life -
A loving heart is a landscape infinite!
Prayer is nothing but love -
Caring for the whole existence in sight!

God is love and love is God
The only expression of eternal affection!
Why devotion equates to love
And love equates to devotion.

Offerings

Only flowing in the river of tears
We can reach the abode of universal dear!
Untying self from inside and outside
Filtering knowledge acquired and inert words
Lessening burden of fruitlessness
Filling heart with kindness
Surrendering self centeredness
Recognizing love as limitless
Observing footprints timeless
Listening silent tunes endless
Never getting lost in vastness
Accepting finite begets infiniteness!
Knowing pains are the way to feel closeness
All sufferings end in Oneness!

Canadian Pride

Song about Canada – written (11/11/2000) and composed (E Phrygian) (The poem was written on the Ferry to Victoria, BC, from Port Angeles, WA, when returning to Canada after staying in US for 14 years, 1987-2000).

O Canada!
What a wonderful beautiful land!
Who always fought –
For peace and just around the world!

From Atlantic to Pacific -
Your graceful wonders abound!
Using science and arts, blending old and new -
Your civilization envy of the world!

Where multiculturalism spreads –
To its fullest extent!
Where democracy stands high –
With your people of great voice!

O Canada!
We will always keep you the great!
O Canada!
We will keep you the great! Always!

Canadian
(Dedicated to all fallen soldiers around the world)

Whether born as Canadian -
Or landed immigrant naturalized in their new homeland
Or refugee found safe home without worries of persecution
They all thank God in private to be Canadian!

As they drive through North America
New York to California, Main to Arizona!
Québec city to Toronto, Sue Saint Marie to Victoria
Stop by Cities, small towns and rest areas
They feel proud whenever travelling in Canada!

When they fly or cruise abroad
See new country meet people culture ashore
Adapt quickly, learn, enjoy and feel at home!
Bring back warmth of love from a world so close
Feel blessed seeing welcoming smile at arriving port!

They feel proud of their strong yet just nation
Confirming soldiers are sent only for peace mission!
Ensuring no one is blaming Canada for aggression
Enjoy dinner and sleep without humiliation!
Hoping Canada leads world with universal vision
Absolutely Canadian without imitation!

Poems by Kolki   About universal well being, peace and love   *Absolutely Humane*

American Pride
(Dedicated to true Democracy without <u>Slavery</u> and <u>Hegemony</u>)

American pride! I felt it –
Visiting the <u>Washington DC Mall</u>!
Enjoying free access to Museums, watching <u>cherry blossoms</u>!
Touring inside <u>Capitol</u> witnessing Congress in session!
As <u>Liberty Bell</u>, <u>Valley Forge</u> –
Reminded past sacrifices and dedication!
Watching <u>George Washington</u> fights for American freedom -
Hungry, sleepless across Potomac in deep winter season!
Accompanied by <u>African, Indian and French</u> fighting Colonialism!

American pride! I felt it -
Listening Lincoln's passionate call to <u>abolish slavery</u>!
Dr. King's <u>arousing speech</u> of a 'Dream World' for everybody!
<u>Malcolm X' visionary voice</u> to end segregations for unity!
Visiting <u>national monuments</u>, <u>parks</u>, <u>galleries</u> and <u>universities</u>!
Driving through country roads exploring <u>boundless sceneries</u>!
Stopping by <u>woods</u>, <u>lakes</u>, <u>oceans</u>, <u>towns</u> in friendly communities!
Hearing <u>national anthem</u> during most Olympic victories!

The pride dampened –
Meeting <u>homeless, hungry, helpless</u> in cities and countryside!
Watching how openly some <u>authority neglect human rights</u>!
<u>Executives earn millions</u> when <u>working poor barely survive</u>!
Military spend billions to guard <u>strategic posts worldwide</u> -
While bridges, roads, parks collect fees and tolls unkind!
The private medicinal care serves well nobles and elites -
Guarding status quo that <u>ignores millions</u> suffer in quiet!
Minorities, elderly, feel humiliated by <u>voter registration plight</u> -
While <u>paperless machines</u> can be made difficult to vote right!

The pride further dampened –
Discovering <u>Prison Industry</u> needs criminal feeds for profits!
<u>Gun violence and homicide</u> make fellow Americans statistics!

American Pride (Cont.)

National Rifles Association breeds militias without registry!
Ghettos overshadow corporate towers exposing hypocrisy!
Discriminations embedded in housing and renting industry!
Lowest minimum wage in the developed world democracies!
Shortest vacations, few working holidays, for many employees!
President gets elected stopping vote counts by Chief Justice!

The pride became distasteful travelling abroad!
Often feeling unwelcome as if America is synonym of horror!
Realizing our leaders are jokes, cartoons, effigies of terror!

Death penalty is an embarrassment for the civilized world!
Wondering what made a pristine country the worst polluter -
Fuelling warships, sorties and vehicles as gas guzzlers!
Observing Defense industry hijacks government for wars!
Soldiers kill civilians, women and children, as invaders!
Reconstruction industries profit as rebuilding contractors!
International Republican Institute acts as global violators!
Injecting soft money and violence for electing feudal powers!

But I still keep the dream alive -
Hoping and praying we recover soon our lost pride!
Being bold, honest and thoughtful to universal rights!
Leading united world for humane global strive!
So help us God again to rise!
As we Celebrate 4th of July enlightened seeing dawn's early light!

Proud itizen
(Dedicated to good old World without border)

I always wanted to be a <u>proud citizen</u>!
Where I could respect my leader as comrade!
Feel good about people with character against violence!
Honesty and humility are the main theme of coherence!

My fate wasn't easy, star wasn't lucky!
As new born democracy converted to market economy!
Violence, militia, agents, promoters, media took over
As natural market, community and freedom disappeared!

God kept me alive as I studied hard with focus -
To gain educative voice against all odds!
Suddenly my first job landed me in USA
The land of <u>Washington</u>, <u>Lincoln</u>, <u>Dr. King</u> and <u>Malcolm X</u>!

After initial excitements, amazements and celebrations -
Soon realized it is <u>no more the product of American Revolution</u>!
My tax money went more to fund military and aid for allies
Than to feed and care for the homeless, helpless and hungry!
Democracy gave in to Supreme <u>Court installed Presidency</u>!
People's voice got defeated by a fiery <u>new anarchy</u>!

Disillusioned, I moved to Canada and became <u>Canadian</u>!
Appreciating values universal, people warmly humanitarian!
Thanked God for the opportunity to taste real freedom!
Finally, I could proudly tell the world I <u>found my home</u>!

Government changed with new election!
Importing greed, voucher, fear, resembling American <u>Neo-Cons</u>!
Disheartened! I looked back to my life and inner self!
Rejoiced! Everything only helped me be a proud world citizen!

Poems by Kolki   About universal well being, peace and love   *Absolutely Humane*

Pro-American
(Dedicated to all American Leaders and Citizens energized with true American Spirit)

Every time I tried to speak like an American for the Americans -
Minority owned majority <u>Media</u> tried to pin me down!
Whether I am also pro-Israeli believe in pre-emptive strikes!
My opinion about Gay, Lesbians and abortion rights!
Which section of America I am speaking for –
Democrats or Republicans!
Whether believe in tax cuts ignoring poor and uninsured millions!
Which issues are important based on my ideology -
Liberal, conservative, passionate conservative or <u>neo-conservative</u>!
Where I stand on trade unions, wars and military cuts!
For Kyoto or status quo believing in environment last!
Whether easy on guns, tough on crimes, pro-death or pro-life!
For more national-debt, deficit spending, retirement age hike!

Never had a chance to speak from my mouth with passion -
Because the analysts talked about it already using intuition!
Feelings in my heart never reached the vast audience
Because they ruined my character with past personal events!
If media mirrored <u>equal opportunity</u> obligations -
Then politicians could focus on issues <u>best for America</u> overall!

If media without analysts had time and patience to listen!
Could read the message straight to people as has been said!
My fellow Americans could think with vision wide and clear!
Recognizing true <u>9/11 plotters</u> running America destroying world!
Silencing citizens with <u>Anthrax</u>, <u>Wire-Taps</u> and '<u>War of Terror</u>'!

Smart

(Dedicated to all who can rise for truth, justice and peace)
[**Without 9/11 Truth, Generations will live with lies endangering our world
– Kolki**]

Since childhood, I was little slow kind except running!
Used to think more than needed before responding!
That made me a fast runner, speed player -
But a slow learner and delayed answerer!

Pressured by parents and peers, tried my best to become smart!
Finished schools and universities learning state of the art!
Discovered how smartness dictates career in the world!
Surpassing honesty, creativity, sincerity and hard work!
Engaged in conflicts to reveal people only acting smart!

As I grew older –
My reactions to chronic world problems became even slower!
Analyzing events more reading between lines undercover!
Watched how we feel secured staying busy with career!
In better car, richer neighbourhood, bigger house and barrier!
Ignoring bigotry, ideology leading to violence and wars!

I slowed down to feel how earth spinning for daily rotation!
Listened to plants, animals, birds, beyond civilized pollution!
Saw God's smiles illuminating dynamic creative evolution!
True smartness is to embrace truth against all humiliation!

Good Neighbor
(Dedicated to neighbourly world)

Say Hi, share a smile
Whenever a neighbour is passing by!
Find out who they are
Inviting all to home for tea or cider!

Exchange holiday greetings
Respect religious beliefs
Ignore political views
Enjoy cheers sharing good news!

Celebrate occasions together
Taste new food and culture!
Spice your life with whatever differs
Feel the joy of united hearts!

Buy Champagne or a cake
Bake some cookies or bread
As neighbours leave or come afresh
Extend good-bye or welcome to celebrate!

Busy with chores, have no time?
Not so well or passing hard time?
Just say hello or wave your hands
So they feel at home harmonized!

Be always nice to your fellow beings!
Known or just new in town site seeing!
Show your kind heart and gentle smile
Lest you never see them again in lifetime!

Violence
(Dedicated to all daily victims of violence around the world)

Violence starts from slaughterhouse!
Moves into a shopping bag!
Comes to the dinner table
Served as delicious meal -
Delighting our face, watering our mouth!

With no sight of killing,
Cry for help, pain and suffering -
Glides into stomach for assimilation
Rests in small intestine for absorption!
Moves to every cell
Finds nest in the brain!
Gradually hardens sensitive mind
Teaches acceptance of abuse, violent crime!

Violence grows with larger appetite
Covered in fashion by peer pressures!
Eliminates childhood ideals and curiosity
Embraces alcohol, tobacco and pornography!
Justifies recreation for civilized being
Including boxing, hunting, racism or drive by shooting!

Violence accompany us leaving school
Crowds' corporate boardrooms!
Applies management science for profits
Downgrading employee salary, security, benefits!

Seeded in teachers, lawyers, storeowners!
Scientists, politicians, labourers or brokers!
Judges, doctors, lawmakers, or law keepers
Displays horrors as convenient measures!

Baptized with Scripture's blessings
Becomes part of a 'Commander in chief'!
Inherits most destructive power

Violence (Cont.)

To fight a war or make a war!

Briefed in secrecy while golfing
Making decision while hunting
Addressing nation at prime time viewing -
Starts a war, justify troops sending!

Submerged in wine and jovial mood
Relaxed with friends inside cozy war room
Precisely delivers missiles, shells, nuclear bombs!
Destroys countries, beings of all forms –
Unaware, unprepared, unarmed, unknown!

Killings
(Dedicated to all who suffer from human killings of convenience, 03/31/2006)

Killings are the beginning of all human sufferings
Taught by Buddha the enlightened king!
Love thy neighbour, Thou shall not kill,
Taught by the son of Bethlehem, Jesus the Nazarene!
Look at the eyes of your slaughter make sure they don't cry
That's how Prophet Muhammad preached far and wide!

Why modern civilized human commit sins -
Killing legal quota of thousands of baby seals!
Seagulls and penguins for meat and fur industry needs!
Slaughtering millions of cows for one Mad Cow Disease!
Destroying ducks and chickens with bird flu terror synthetic
For competitive advantage of global poultry industries!
Poaching elephants, rhinos, monkeys, tigers and chimps!
Hunting grizzly, quail, cuckoo, pheasants, deer and geese!
Attacking countries beyond borders killing citizens at peace!

No matter how good war technology some scientists develop!
Nuclear bombs, bunker busters or daisy cutters!
Biological, chemical, weapons or lethal lasers!
Earth penetrating bombs, biotech bacteria and virus!

No matter how humanely military deliver
Deadly missiles as carefully filmed surgical strikes!
Or frontal combat of bullets and machine gun fights!
Killing own kind is nothing but brutal murderous sight!

Hunters may publicise with humane, gentle and kind masks
Hunting with clubs, riffles, knives, arrows, shot guns!
Knowing well that killing is never 'Kosher'
Only inflicts cruel pains to helpless innocent sufferers!

Lost Sound
(Dedicated to pristine world)

Ever wonder –
What happens to all extra sounds we create in this world?
From daily chores to mining, logging, building, industrial efforts!
Due to entertainment, sirens, traffic horns and public concerts!
Running ships, airplanes, fighter jets, trains, buses and trucks!
Blasting bombs in wars and testing nuclear weapons
Pounding steel beams to bedrocks or planned demolitions!

Sound propagates in the air as compression and depression!
Its energy follows the law of conservation!
Thus every sound we create will propagate in some form!
Travelling somewhere around the globe waiting for action!

Resonance of union of many lost sound waves
Can result in catastrophic natural consequences!
Severely affecting weather with unpredictable disturbances
Including storms, tornados, cyclones and hurricanes!

We must be careful for the endless sound we create –
Lest they come back to haunt us and our children!

Baptism-Initiation

Human always wondered about the world around!
The sky above, the oceans, beings underground!
But most of their simple queries remained unanswered!
Despite vast knowledge, academic and corporate, gathered!
Discussions among colleagues, friends, networking with peers!
Eventually led them to have faith in a God of fear!

I had seen people being initiated!
Friends, colleagues, baptised in faiths inherited!
Watched helplessly as many turn inwardly limited!
Kept myself away un-baptised, un-initiated!

Realization comes with vision unlimited!
Recognizing Initiation happens throughout life so many ways!
Rebuilding faith in learning as an evolutionary process!
Observing parents, siblings, family, friends, in neighbourly village!
Watching plants, animals, birds, insects and fishes!
Feeling seasons with transitory sun, moon, stars and planets!

Message of dawn bombarding earth each day!
Irrespective of Baptism by Gurus or Priests in temples and churches!
To help us ascend over limitations embracing universal acceptance!

Faith

Peter is a Christian who believes in Jesus as the Saviour!
Prasad is a Hindu who worships Vishnu as Lord!
Rahaman is a Muslim who prays to Allah as the only God!
Abhya is Buddhist who serves sentient beings reading Tripitaka!
Adar is a Hebrew who practices Judaism in Synagogue!
....
They were living in harmony in same community!
Doing their daily work for family and charity!
Without much worrying about ideology or supremacy!
Enjoying life well in prosperity, cordially extending hospitality!

Until foreigners invaded their country to make them free!
They saw destruction of their land with bombing spree!
Peaceful co-existence became nightmares in autocracy!
Enriching few betrayers as the new authority of democracy!

Spring

Earth is warming up since winter solstice!
For the kingdoms in Northern Hemisphere!
Days are getting longer sun brighter
Birds are visible in large numbers
Animals are out to soothe hunger
Whatever makes a meal can't wait any longer!

Human dresses getting lighter
Vegetables on the shelves grow older
Parks and trails traffic getting heavier
Snows are melting in temperature warmer
Water is rushing through everywhere
Daffodils and tulips are bringing cheers
Pigs shadow confirms its spring no more winter!

Window
(Written, March 29, 2006)

From my very childhood –
I was fond of windows!
Windows in my playhouse
Windows in my study room
Window seat on public bus
Window seat in my class!
Window seat on airplane
Eating by the window in restaurants!
Why bought houses with many windows
Or installed new ones for feeling mellow!
Suddenly God gave me another window!
Which seems to be moving with my shadow!
Showing me the world with a vision anew
Beyond my imaginations and preconceived views!
Making me a lone spectator
In a world full of actors!

Poems by Kolki   About universal well being, peace and love   *Absolutely Humane*

Father's Day
(Dedicated to all who lost father, spouse, child to illegal supremacy wars)
[Debaathization is genocide of 200,000+ Iraqis and Detalibanization is genocide of 50,000+ Afghans! Kolki]

As the Self Proclaimed leaders of the new axis power
Celebrate Father's Day in private dinner
Thousands of Iraqis-Afghanis are without father!
Mother and child mourning in frustration and despair -
Caused by brutal Neocon military ambition of terror!
Destroying beloved country, people and infrastructure!
While many friends and family miss fallen soldiers!

As world maintain laws punishing criminals and violators
The new axis leaders still enjoying freedom with honour!
Hiding behind Al-virus in cyberspace and television!
Suppressing Rule of Law and Proof of Conviction!
Proudly encouraging Debaathization, Detalibanization -
The crusading campaign for worldwide genocidal mission!

Silence is betrayal which may haunt us all forever!
Ignoring history only empower real criminals of wars!
If we don't stand by friends who are felons and murderers -
Why must we side with invading mass murders?
Imagine yourself as a would be father
Anxiously waiting in hospital for her arrival to deliver
But she has been shot by occupying military –
at a check point barrier!

The feudal power survives and succeeds only breeding fear!
Using divisive tools depriving world from universal prayer!
Let us unite as father, child and would be father!
Stop crusaders from taking us to wars against each other!
Unmask their deceptive guise framing patsy with rumours!
Revive universal fatherhood ending all politics of smear!
Celebrate Father's Day aloud confirming unified cheer!

Son

Son brings joy, happiness, hope of new generation!
After months of worries, dreams, since conception!
To help sustain life's miraculous journey of the new born –
Parents guide him to ride the waves –
from childhood to graduation!
With loving care, blessings and education!

As the son attains manhood crossing barriers of competition!
Passion of love encourages new exploration!
Leading to discovery of life-long companion!
While enriching parents with a daughter in possession!
Bringing in possibilities of grand daughter and grand son!
A son is the symbol of eternal creation!

Loneliness

We come on earth and leave alone!
But the attachments during journey aboard
Make us afraid to be alone!
Keeping our minds busy as we dig holes!

It is the loneliness -
That gives us a chance to feel we are never alone!
As most embraces daily chores of stressful union!
Some hear the message of freedom -
Convert inertia of rest to inertia of motion
Making the best use of human creation!

Happiness

Happiness is in one's mind!
Some feel it in crowded bars and coffee house
Some in temple, some in solitude
Learned reading novels and book
Others among their family at home!

Some listening to good music
Some singing God's glory
Most find it in being loved
Many in activism for peace and nature!

Some enjoys happiness eating good food
Some serving others in distress or in need
Most enjoy happiness in harmony and peace
But a few find them –
in inflicting destruction unleashed!

Pain

Every time I had pain
I used to suffer!
Whether it's from losing a game
Or unexpected score in exam
Or separating with a loved one
Or someone suffering from social unjust!

Heart always ached choking voice losing breath!
Made me wonder through empty streets at night
Looking at the sky may be emptiness knows why
Dearest dreams become dear making us cry
Nearest soul evades bondage on the fly
Some people undermine others with hatred and lies!

Life went on; eyes became dry, heart normal
Some innocence lost others emboldened
Bad news made me sad but not heart broken
Mind knows the limit beyond which we are helpless
Pains are nothing but tools for surviving experience!

Worth
(Dedicated to Labour Day with a hope for worldwide Humanhood)

Life is worth –
When my waste collectors
Shake hands, hug as friend!
Mail deliverers wave hands
As passing by without my mail!
Cashiers at the grocery line smile
Happy to see once again for a little while!

Life is worth –
When neighbour knocks on door to say Hi
Vehicles stop for pedestrians without a sigh!
Politicians are thoughtful, truthful and kind
Universal care resonating human minds!

Life is worth –
When sun comes out in the morning
Bright in smog free blue sky!
Trees are around abound welcoming
Birds are flying free in flock busy nesting
Animals grazing playing mating without worries!

Life is worth –
When able bodied people are working happily
Without losing benefit and security
Contracts getting renewed proactively
People can collect welfare proudly!

Life is worth –
When world leaders are communicating
No country is under attack or attacking
No soldier away from home except peace-keeping
Enjoying dinner knowing no one goes to bed hungry
Sleeping at night assuring no homeless suffering!
Dreaming sweet dreams finally God is smiling!

Nightmares
(Dedicated to Tsunami, Earthquake, War and Political Victims)

Nightmares are worst dreams
Which seize us unaware in deep sleep!
It is very real until it ends
Waking us up with a sigh of relief!
Scared, sweating or shivering, still bewildered
We thank God it wasn't real after all!

But often nightmares are real
Happening in broad daylight or at night!
Eyes feel hypnotized, mind in disbelief
Won't ever bring back solace ending sleep!

It happens when Tsunami hits coastline
Or an earthquake devastate normal life
Or one's lover is sleeping in someone else's arms
Or terrorists blowing up building, train or bus
Or underdogs suffering –
from irresponsible tax and service cuts
Or invading military marching on with brutal adventures -
Killing, abusing, scorching –
everything in their ignorant victory path!

Coffee

I was sleepy
You woke me up
I was yawning
You stirred me up
I was down
You made me high
I was depressed
You brought back my strength
I was cold
You gave me warmth
I was lonely
You made me feel homey
I needed sleep
You kept me awake
I was tired
You let me work harder
I saw you as friend
You made be en-slaved
You helped my dreams come true
But the body can't enjoy just falling through!

In Vain
(Dedicated to a united world, co-existing peacefully in diversity)

In vain -
A seed which couldn't germinate!
A bud that didn't bloom into flower!
A fish couldn't swim freely into water!
A bird in a cage at the mercy of the owner!
An animal in the laboratory away from nature!
An unfortunate prey waiting to be slaughtered!
A pet lived alone among people neutered!
A body deprived of romance leading to heir!
A foetus aborted for convenience of irresponsible lovers!
Eyes without vision to see everything everywhere!
Ears which couldn't listen to sounds traveling in the air!
A tongue without luck to quench thirst and relieve hunger!
Hands which couldn't work and grow a plant with care!
A mouth which couldn't express joy of freedom in love!
A mind that never wondered about grandeur of universe!
A nose could never enchant brain with fragrance of flower!

In vain -
A heart which never fell in love with compassion!
A soul untouched by others' sufferings and celebrations!
A leader who couldn't speak truth under oath for illusion!
A voice that never rose against war and oppression!
A life eliminated by abusive violence of violation!
A human which couldn't realize universal notes of Salvation!

Poems by Kolki   About universal well being, peace and love   *Absolutely Humane*

Vegetarian World
(Dedicated toward a healthy and peaceful world in communion)

Then God said, "I give you every seed-bearing plant,
On the face of the whole earth -
And every tree that has fruit with seed in it -
They will be yours for food". (**Genesis 1:29**)
"You who have compassion for a lamb -
"Shall be the shepherd of my people Israel" (Exodus Rabbah)
Killing is the beginning of all human sufferings!" (Buddha)
" Thou Shall Not Kill –
Man shall reap that which he hast sown.
So be it the Law of Justice" (Jesus)
"There is not an animal on earth,
Nor a bird that flies on its wings –
But they are communities like you." *(The Quran, 6:38)*

Imagine if world was still vegetarian!
Billions of cows won't be raised to be slaughtered!
No chicken or rabbit head severed!
No pig, goat, lamb butchered!
No fish out of water!
Food is always Halal and Kosher!

Earth won't be polluted with blood and left over!
Bazaar and Market won't smell like rotten corpse!
Good health would cut down nation's health care costs!
Fishing boats would ferry for commerce and pleasure stops!
Seagulls won't crowd ocean beaches, neither shark!
Meat industry won't destroy grains causing global hunger!

No one would terrorise as hunters and poachers!
Birds would fly happily with family in cheers!
Natural grazers would graze horizon as family together!
Flesh burning smell won't pollute parks, restaurants and bars!
Forests would be greener without accidental fires!
Rumours and fears won't drive us to wars!
Peace activists will sleep well without nightmares!

Vegetarian World (Cont.)

If we still could hear, God's message loud and clear –
"Behold my child – It is late but not beyond the border!
To live in a Vegetarian World enjoying heavenly pleasures!
Coexisting with fellow beings without hatred, <u>violence</u> and fear!

Spirit of Victoria
(Dedicated as song composed in E-Minor for the Victoria, BC)

Victoria, Oh Victoria!
Beautiful, Friendly, Victoria!
In enchanting British Columbia,
Capital City Victoria!

Victoria, Oh Victoria!
On the strait of Juan De Fuca!
Mountain-view, lake, ocean surrounds,
Year round pleasant Victoria!

Victoria, Oh Victoria!
Modern, yet charming Victoria!
Loving and caring Victoria,
Pride of mighty Canada!

What is New Year!
(Dedicated to loving and caring world)

Earth is rotating on its own axis!
Revolving at thirty kilometres per second velocity!
Around our Sun seemingly glowing eternally!
One rotation makes a day we all cherish!
Passing through deep space staying on path relentlessly!
Bringing us in dawn, morning, noon, twilight and evening!

Eight other planets moving around the Sun together!
Almost in the same plane inside Sun's celestial sphere!
As delicate orbital path maintains distance from each other!
Along the circumference of nearly 940 million kilometres!
Asteroid belt is just additional set of bodies to care!

Sun is rotating on own axis maintaining dynamic equilibrium!
Revolving around Galactic centre along with billions of stars!
Drifting through intergalactic space in a second 220 kilometres!
Traversing 200 million light years as solar year!

As Earth moves around the Sun!
Vernal and autumnal equinox bring spring and autumn!
Solstices take us through winter and summer!
Driving a careful revolution around the Sun!
Still safe, unharmed, intact and a place for fun!
Certainly the best reason to celebrate with open arms!
Ignoring petty conflicts, ignorant supremacist scars!
Let us celebrate New Year with universal cheers!

Universal Celebration!!
(Dedicated to the citizens of the world)

Happy New Year!
Happy New Year!
Happy New Year to all my friends!
Happy New Year to everyone else -
Around the world.

One more year passed by –
With the flow of our time –
Adding memories,
Knowledge and love!

Many children born -
Throughout the world!
Need peace and love to grow -
To see a better tomorrow!

As we celebrate –
With fireworks and champagne!
Let's not forget -
It's not for everyone!

So, let us take this vow –
From this very day!
We will see new years -
Where everyone celebrates!

Fallen Leaves

Its end of autumn!
Fall in most winter land!
Deciduous trees –
Ash, Birch, Poplar, Walnut, Russian-Olives
Oak, Willow, Maple, Apple, Plum, Hazelnut, Peach
Shed leaves sealing twig tips in fear
For up coming cold, storm and snowy winter!
Saying goodbye to coloured family in grief
Hoping a joyous reunion during next spring!

People are usually fed up
To see sudden leaves pile ups
Over their dear lawn, garden and shrubs
Blow them away with noisy leaf blower!

I am still old fashioned extra-mundane
Enjoy raking enormous volume for days
Shed from endangered poetic Gary Oak trees
Looking at them and listening to their stories!

Rolling through the lawn
They move along driveway down hill
Singing their tales of spring, summer and fall
Most sweet reminiscences after all!

Mamma Didn't Know
(Dedicated to Mother's Day)

Mamma didn't know –
First time I was swimming with friends -
Almost drowned myself crying for help!
That I missed her when in school all day!
Felt empty inside every time she was away -
Visiting uncles or close friends even for a day!
Food didn't taste good, game wasn't same
As if world was stalling toward sudden end!

Mamma didn't know –
I almost choked to death inhaling first cigarette!
That teacher punished me for other's misdeeds by mistake!
Opponent beat me badly for victory in a friendly game!
My pain seeing silent lover became someone else' friend!
My fear seeing neighbour killed by militia for political gain!
My frustration often Government invent terrorism for campaign!

Mamma didn't know –
How much I cried in disbelief even as adult!
Knowing diplomacy hides truth in professional world!
Defense Industries make profit from the horror of War!
Politicians lie under oath to hide supremacy terror!
Religion writes prophecies justifying killings with fear!

Mamma didn't know –
That I thanked her every time I cooked my meal!
Apologized for past complaints I didn't mean!
When the noise of daily chores quiet down
Competition for survival didn't take me out of town -
My mind wanted to serve her the way she served me!
And rest in her lap like a child listening mythical stories!

Angels

[Written, March 20, 2005 - Dedicated to Naomi, a pure and true loving soul who flew away before adulthood)]

Angels are not dropped from the sky!
They are born among us and can't fly!
Angels grow up as a symbol of wisdom and love
Ignoring most complications from our industrial world!

As we, humans, keep ourselves submerged -
With modern chores, party and fun!
Angels work silently with smile
Making our lives worry free and worthwhile!

Good souls only come to earth for a short while!
Reminding us the goodness we all have inside!
Showing us the power of love over hatred –
Illuminate the joy of freedom in co-existence!
Enlighten minds to rise above doubts and fear
'God means only good', our universal dear!

Marie

(Dedicated to Earth-Angels who resemble Marie, written 9/2/2004)

I called you Marie –
Because I know it makes you happy
Feeling pride in instincts so divine-motherly!

I called you Marie –
Because I may not have a chance
To say it again
If tomorrow Earth finds itself
Without a Sun!

Time has changed!
The world is no more the same –
Since New Testament
Found enlightenment in crucifixion and crusades
Depriving 'West' of all future prophets!

In the age of Military science and commerce!
Even Marie could find it difficult –
Remaining virgin as adult
Bringing in Jesus to this world!

As I still breathe and speak
I want to see you merry!
Despite all modern limitations
You could still be Marie!

Jingle Bell (New)

Jingle Bells Jingle Bells Jingle All the Way
O What a Fun to Celebrate Christmas in True (Old) Way!

Loving each other
Caring for every soul
Sharing this world of ours in every which way!

Keeping world safe
Respecting (to) everyone's rights
No arms conflict among us
Just peace in harmony!

Eid ul-Fitr

(Dedicated to all who have been suffering from 21st Century crusades against humanity)

The fasting comes to an end
After thirty long days
Re-enforcing base's fourth pillar
Experiencing the climax of Ramadan
On the night of power
The dawn calls to celebrate **Eid ul-Fitr!**
Embracing each other saying 'Eid Mubarak'!

Eid is the time for brotherhood and unity
Establishing peace through forgiveness and mercy
Overcoming all fear with passion and feelings
Thanking God Almighty for all blessings!

Let the fast end all evil Ignorant-Hostility
Spreading the message of moral victory!
Reminding Jihad is purifying mind-body
Joyous celebration of the achievement of enhanced piety!

Vegetarian
(Dedicated to healthy word)

I used to love meat!
I was raised among poultry and fish!
Nothing could excite my hunger best
Than just thought of curried egg and omelette!

Slowly I kept on losing
Appetite for meat and poultry
Egg was still favourite,
Until the look became detesting!

Stuck in a meat based society
My sudden conversion wasn't easy!
At times it felt like self-defeating
Until I learn my own way of cooking!

Used spices for the flavour I was missing
Cut vegetables that appear appetizing
A good ripe fruit made my mouth watering
Meat substitutes tasted great without smelling!

Even my egg-less desert rice pudding -
Became famous like Grandma's cooking!
Overall it made me a better human being
Ready to preach for peace and vegetarianism!

Poems by Kolki   About universal well being, peace and love   *Absolutely Humane*

Illegal Immigrants (Aliens)
(Dedicated to one world where people serve stranger with 'old world' hospitality)

[Every country must have immigration rules to prevent chaos and ensure security! But it is time to ask few politicians and analysts, spreading hate crimes, where are they from? Kolki]

If India guarded its ancient border against illegal Aryans!
Natives would still be Shaivites evolving Neandarthals!
If China treated strangers fearing illegal immigrants
Marko Polo couldn't tell West existence of that wonderland!
If Scythians couldn't ruin ancient India and Hurians Babylon -
Mesopotamia to India still probably be Indo-Iranian!
If Mark Twain had to worry about his legal status -
World would be without his fascinating Travelogues!

If we really try to reopen the can of worms –
Natives may find most of us as illegal arrivals!

With barbed wires and armed forces vigilant –
Pilgrims could never reach US mainland!
Slavery couldn't destroy Africa and Africans!
Mexican would be still proud as Mayans -
As Texan, New Mexican, Floridian, Arizonian and Californian!
Aryans never ruled India as Vedic custodian!
Hittites couldn't destroy Mitannis, Hyksos Egyptians!
Britain would be still a laid back Celtic land!
Australia, New Zealand would still be land of aboriginals!
America would be still pristine under Native Americans!
Israelites couldn't massacre in peaceful Canaan!
India would be void of wrath of Brahminic Scythians!
"Philistine" would mean "native of "Palestine"!
Rome would be ruled by Romans void of Vatican!
Potato famine couldn't destroy Irish farmers!
Ireland would be a land of united communal culture!
White Huns never destroyed Persia marring silk route with fear!

List can go on but the point is obvious!

Illegal Immigrants (Aliens)

If we coexist without fighting who came first -
World would be living in peace as one happy world!
Enjoying varieties without worries ignoring <u>prophetic</u> religion -
There will be always enough for everyone!

Co-existence

(Written for the children composed for Piano in C-Major)

Plants and animals
(And) Birds and Ocean lives –
One and complete evolution!

Together sharing
And caring for each other –
We can keep world one and complete!
Co-exist in peace and harmony!

Bunny
(Dedicated to meaningful Easter around the world)

We are rabbits!
Many adore us as Bunnies, Easter Bunnies!
We grow naturally -
As a sign of age old fertility!

Our needs are very simple!
Green grass, water and air without polution!
Open space, open yard, not concrete jungle!
Your mowed lawn is only half good for our nutrition!
Because we need the tip of the new grass for metabolism!

For many we are tasty delite!
A pest for the urban developing sites!
Every time you build on earth we suffer!
Acid rain and pesticides deform our heir!
So please help us from the bottom of your hearts!
That you always find real rabbit eggs for Easter!
Making generations to come happy together!
Celebrating festivities being fruitful on Earth!

Earth

(Dedicated to dear Earth the only living place in the Universe we know of)

Oh Mother Earth!
Bestow upon us the energy of fire!
Help us rise above shyness, greed and fear!
Warm our hearts as we breathe truth so dear -
Make our mind fearless, thoughtful and clear!

Oh! Loving Power, reveal your universal message ancient!
Alas! We fight wars and destroy Eco system so delicate –
Despite being creative and intelligent!
Inspire us to co-exist once again in non-violence!

Oh dearest Living Planet!
Rise and energize us with your evolving secret!
Help us overcome poverty, supremacy and global hazards -
Making us work with selfless love and care!

Natural Rhythm
(Dedicated to a Secular World)
[Fundamentalism keeps the momentum of evolution whether in Physics, Chemistry, Mathematics or Religion! Without it science becomes stagnant applied technology, religion becomes ritualistic anarchy! It is true <u>Baptism</u> which makes one born again, encourage science and religion to seek truth and nothing less! The only threat to world peace comes from private <u>militarism</u> which is against rule of law, proof of conviction and gun control giving rise to private militia, a convenient instrument often used by corrupt intelligence, military and judiciary to silence oppositions for Supremacy! <u>Kolki</u>]

Walking in a noisy city -
Certainly better with Walkman CD!
But one rejuvenates mind body –
With natural rhythm harmonized in simplicity!

One two three four! Five six seven eight!
Nine ten eleven twelve! Thirteen fourteen fifteen sixteen!

Do Re Mi Fa! So La Ti Do!
Do Ti La So! Fa Mi Re Do!

Sa Re Ga Ma! Pa Dha Ni Sa!
Sa Ni Dha Pa! Ma Ga Re Sa!

Dha Dhin Dhin Dha! Dha Dhin Dhin Dha!
Na Tin Tin Ta! Tete Dhin Dhin Dha!

Left right left – ! Left right left – !
Left right left right! Left right left - !

<u>Thou shall not kill</u>! Thou shall not kill!
Love thy neighbour! Love thy enemy!

Natural Rhythm (Cont.)

Moses! Moses! Moses! Moses!
Aadonai is coming again!

Hare Krishna Hare Krishna Krishna Krishna Hare Hare!
Hare Raama Hare Raama Raama Raama Hare Hare!

Allah Hu Akbar - ! Allah Hu Akbar - !
Subhan Allah! Subhan Allah! Allah Hu Akbar - !

Amitabhaa! Amitabha!
Namo Namo Amitabha!

Ek Omkar - ! Ek Omkar - !
Wahe Guru! Ek Omkar - !

Love and care! Love and Care!
World is better together!

Trinity

Brahma, Vishnu, Shiva
Represent God's three epical expressions!
Like Father, Son, Holy Ghost
In Christian faith and imaginations!

Though trinity in combination
Bring about God's total manifestation
God exist in the middle as abstraction
Maintains constant rhythm of harmonization!

Science can help visualise abstraction
Attributing trinity among fundamental particles
Universal neutron, proton and electron
Resembling epical and Christian characterization!

Neutron-Father the basic particle of the universe
Splits into energetic Electron and Proton mass
Excited by sub-atomic vibration instantaneous
Separates and recombines inside nucleus!

Proton almost retains the mass of Neutron-Brahma-Father
Electron is mostly energy as Holy Ghost-Shiva!
Thus Vishnu-Son maintains the body of the universe
Shiva-Holy Ghost enacts creative evolutionary power!

God is the heat behind eternal primeval vibration
That causes neutron to split into electron and proton
Helps create Son and Holy Ghost from Father
Exposes Vishnu and Siva from Brahma
Preserving abstract magic of love forever
As Allah, Buddha, Rama, Krishna!

Radha
(Dedicated to wife Radha)

Radha is the reason for Krishna's love!
Which flows throughout the universe -
To embrace her embodiment
That transforms from finite to limitless!

They become one for a moment
Only to break apart as male and female
To enjoy depth of passion in unification -
And intense longing during separation!

She is the cause of all relation
Why neutrons give rise to atoms
Dancing as spontaneous atomic vibration
Atoms combine as molecules
Inspired by Krishna consciousness
Residing in Radha's faithful existence!

Their union and separation
Is the cause of all causes
All creation and evolution!
Krishna is the heat behind cosmic consciousness
Radha contains that heat!
Krishna is Paramatma, Supreme soul, Brahman
Radha is the 'Atman' in Paramatma!
Their spontaneous act of love, material and spiritual -
Maintains eternal dynamic equilibrium!

Electromagnetics!
(Dedicated to all scientific innovations)

God came on Earth as Maxwell
To give us the universal equations!
Only to realize -
Humans are not ready for assimilation!

Heaviside, the only son of God,
Brought the message organized and simplified!
Scientists cheered being enlightened
While military realized the message of dominance!

Engineers promised quick applications
With assumptions, approximations, for implementation!
Mathematics evolved with new equations -
Burying truth farther under complications!

Computers brought the hope of resolution -
But scientists needed super computation!
In a race to compute gamma, s-matrices
Just like detecting new bacteria, viruses!

Computers, exhausted inverting huge matrices
Bestow upon us results and inferences!
Blending assumptions, approximations and truncations,
Reveal new graphs, visions and animations!

World claps as scientists graduate
And some win Nobel Prize for achievements!
Volumes of transactions and proceedings increase
Displaying new products, and claims in conferences!

Electromagnetics! (Cont.)

Scientists retire, engineers end career, with morale high
Look at the medals, publications, and enjoy the blue sky
Yet, go to graves with a big sigh -
Why, how, and why!

Churning

Churning of the ocean is not the ocean on Earth!
It is the churning of the cosmic ocean of the universe!
That created galaxies, then stars, then planets far apart
Using creative forces and recipes of eternal herbs!

The ancient human knowledge got diluted in history!
As invading forces created myths and mysteries!
Divided the world to conquer and rule mastering slavery
Hiding truth and knowledge creating fear of misery!

Assigning goodness to Gods and Goddesses of the invaders
While labelling evilness to oppressed demons the sufferers!
The gospel of creation learned by sages 'the wise listeners'!
Became story of fighting for the possession of eternal nectar!

OM

The sound Om (Aum) of Big Bang spreading everywhere!
With its derivatives higher and higher
As darkness, light, emptiness and atmosphere
Creating stars, galaxies and universal network!
Impacting all as waves of creative power!

We see it bright as the sun light!
We feel it tuned down by the darkness of night!
We exclaim it at the dawn in horizons
We appreciate it as it changes seasons!

We hear it when something catches fire!
In drum beats, blowing wind and steaming water!
In heart beats, touches, scratching and choir!
In speeches, music, shouts, songs and loving desires!
In rain drops, snow showers and rhymes of nature!
In water falls, birds call, in sufferings and cheers!

When lightening strikes, thunder roars, storms whisper on trees!
Volcano erupts, bomb blasts, waves pound on beach!
As realization in loving hearts and vision beyond reach -
Silent message of Om in souls evolve in life primitive!
As atom vibrates, seeds germinate, foetus conceived!

Mantra-Yagna

The name India reminds people of ancient times
Early morning chanting in holy rivers and shrines
Meditating saints uttering mantra in mountain caves
Monkeys, elephants, cows roaming free without fence
Wild bamboo fluty tunes charming dangerous snakes!

Mantra became part of ritual losing original significance
Imbibing repeated invasions and related segregations!
Caste system made Priesthood well guarded profession
Burying ancient knowledge of interstellar conversation!

Mantras are syntax for universal communication!
Invented by Sages realizing nature of cosmic vibrations!
They only become effective with perfect pronunciation!
Synchronizing tongue, vocal chord and stomach air chamber
Converts sound waves to electromagnetic for transfer!
While meditation prepare one as conscious receiver!

Developed as hymns by indigenous Brahmin scientists
Documented by Aryans using script Sanskrit
Precisely compiled as Veda a universal epic!
Attuned with energy - magnetic, electric, heat and delight
Hymns were sung for orderly life with spiritual spice!

Resembling science of packet switching network -
Mantras start with a header ending in trailer!
Sounding 'Om', 'Namah', 'Swaha', 'Swadha', 'Namahstute'
Guiding message embedded for destination intended!
As stored energy of Mantra propagates
Exciting universal modes using bandwidth as needed!

Right mantras when pronounced prolonged in chorus
Can cause enough disturbances in surrounding atmosphere -
Initiating modulation ending in storm, clouds, even rain!
Relieving sufferings from drought illness and pain!

Mantra-Yagna (Cont.)

Mantras themselves can render local communication!
But require 'Yagna- the fire' for long distant transmission!
Performed at the base of a pyramidal horn!
Modulated by the heat of burning offerings in 'Havan' –
Sonic energy rides on optical carrier to celestial destinations!

Conservative
(Dedicated to true united democracy that leads to united growth of Humankind)

[How much more shall we divide us embracing labels of Conservatives, Liberals, Gays, Lesbians, etc.? Most human actions are spontaneous reactions in an effort to adjust with surroundings beyond control. Labeling only enforces status quo hindering natural evolution. <u>Kolki</u>]

In a world so ideologically divisive -
Where politicians join opposition party following Victory -
Driving a nail through the heart of Multi-Party <u>democracy</u>!
Media label people as Gay, Lesbian, Heterosexual or homophobic –

Rightist, Leftist, Socialist, Communist or Fundamentalist -
Encourage campaign side track issues with endless rhetoric!
A few who value family and goodness in humanity -
Often get characterized as conservative!
Making election a mockery of choosing candidates so <u>illusive</u>!

I adore relationship and freedom of joyous union –
Why against commercial pornography, prostitution and abortion!
My dream is to share universal affection -
Ending all known barrier of discrimination!

I label the <u>killing</u> machines in all forms -
As the true and only <u>evil</u> to loving earthly norms!
I believe in things 'We the people' can do better -
Guarantying, for all, good health, education and shelter!

I recognize animals and birds were here -
Before human invaded Earth with alien power!
I envision Dinosaurs never ruled the Earth -
Just coexisted in their natural habitat!

I experienced hunger being angry -
Why never wants to see anybody hungry!
I survived bitter cold nights in campsite -
Why always cry seeing homeless by the road side!

Conservative (Cont.)

I don't vote for a party that fights–
To deprive others of their basic rights!
I avoid culture that feels pride –
Getting morally degraded, mean and wild!

I am against all wars -
Unless we are attacked by invaders!
I believe a true <u>patriot</u> -
Can never send another beyond border!

You may call me conservative or <u>altruist</u>!
Even label me as liberal, socialist or extremist!
Knowing well my thoughts, prayers, efforts and campaign -
Only meant to recover goodness in being humane!

Fallen Soldiers
(Dedicated to all worldwide fallen soldiers and victims of aggression)
[**Imagine a <u>Prime Minister</u> or <u>President</u> died and media <u>couldn't cover</u>!
Certainly life of Allied soldiers are cheaper than the politicians! Kolki**]

My fellow world citizens -
Fallen as soldiers or by soldiers!
Your parents and friends would miss you forever!
Politicians would shed crocodile tears -
As they attend news briefings and fund raising dinners!
Many editorials would use you to raise patriotic fever -
Some would honestly write to stop the menace of wars!
You can be assured of my heartiest and helpless prayers!

I tried very hard as a normal citizen -
Ignoring personal pleasures, family and friends!
To take my peace messages using my <u>voice and pen</u> -
Informing leaders, politicians, journalists, ambassadors of UN!
Feeling urgency to save you all from sudden cruel end!
But they mostly fell in deaf ears or bought humiliation –
Without much gain!

Politicians were not by your side when you were dying in pain!
Media analysts were preaching virtues of strategic gains!
But my mind was always with you –
Like a concerned family or friend!
Couldn't enjoy life wondering why military is not humane!
Rest assured I will keep on dreaming to bring you that day
When soldiers won't fight just exchange flowers bouquet!

Journalist
(Dedicated to united journalists around the world)

A journalist should not bear any label!
Whether Pro-Conservative or Pro-Liberal -
Pro-Democrats, Pro-Green or Pro-Republican -
Pro-Labour, Pro-Gay or Pro-Lesbian!
Pro-West, Pro-Israel or Pro-Palestine!
The only title seems appropriate is pro-human!

Labelling only divides people with burden of bearing!
Truth becomes partisan interpretation illusive!
The irritation of stickiness from coated adhesive
Leads to <u>yellow journalism</u> of infinite gossips!

A journalist should always back fellow journalists!
Must never look for news source with profit motives!
Must not give in to kidnapping, beheading by terrorists!
Knowing they could very well be disguise of imperialists!

A journalist must not be afraid of universalism!
Which is beyond all goodness of socialism and capitalism!
The only thing must be exposed is any form of Neo-ism!
Feeling proud they hold the key to democratic humanism!

Dying
(Dedicated to all who suffer for military Supremacy)

A small pet bird is dying -
Owner parent holding in arm crying
Giving her comfort and care of family
Making her last moments felt much loving!

A pet cat or dog is dying -
Owner parent praying and rushing
Hoping vet can cure with magic
Feeling helpless on the way to clinic!

A baby is dying -
Parents called ambulance with utmost urgency
Sobbing on the way to hospital constantly praying
Begging God's mercy in exchange for everything!

A deer is dying -
. Hunter's bow went through her neck injuring
The noble achiever joyous celebrating
Worrying more for expensive bow before bagging!

An invading army is advancing -
Killing and destroying everything
Making hospital beds overflowing
Helpless doctors watching patients suffering
Until Missiles hit hospital burying all pain abruptly!

World citizens are sleeping or working happily -
Superpower military is planning next attack covertly
Listening posts are updating base instantly
Which house, city, country can be grounded remotely!

Peace
(Dedicated to a peaceful Earth filled with virtues of truth, sharing and caring)

Earth wants peace!
Earth deserves peace to stay beautiful!
Earth needs peace to make all being fruitful!
Earth warrants peace right now, she is Frightful!

She is trembling being hit by thousands pound bombs –
Missiles, shells, mines inflicting wounds over all!
Tanks rolling over scratching her pristine body!
She can't breathe in pollution of explosives!
Created by Fuel, Napalm and depleted uranium so toxic!

Fighter jets dropping bombs to 'Shock and Awe'!
War ships and submarines sending missiles innumerable!
Dangerous Stealth just following the path of annihilation –
Releasing cluster bombs and bunker busters killing all forms!

Nobody will know the real loss and destruction –
Of human being, animal, desert life, forest and civilization –
Which have been turned into debris, dust and ashes –
Beyond the reach of all statistics in history classes!

Life Is Simple
(Song in D major, dedicated to sharing world)

Life used to be too simple
World used to be beautiful
Food used to be plentiful -
Sharing, caring meaningful.

There was competition
But, there were few duplication
(We used to have competition
Without too many duplication….for song)
No free-trade implication -
Import-export was for salvation.

There was no corporation
No self proclaimed civilization -
No market manipulation -
Mutually helpful transactions.

There were no enforced partitions
No artificial divisions
Human culture and civilization -
Followed natural limitation.

Stock Market
(Dedicated to true free market)
(Abstract: World wars were fought whenever market collapsed closing the financial institutions! If market is free, why do we need FED Chairman and speculators for constant manipulation? May be, its time to review if manipulated stock market is the only 21st Century financial tool in the world?)

The bell rings each morning -
Except on weekends or holidays!
Signalling the opening of the market -
In the heart of most crowded cities.

Traders rush in to make their bids (day) -
As millions of shares change invisible hands!
Making it a bull market or bear market -
Just like the happiness and sorrow of life!

The market grows on good ROI (return on investment) -
. And shrinks when workers salaries go high!
The market hates full employment -
Fearing inflation may rise!
And it loves underemployment -
When workers work for less with a smile!

Politicians always worry about the market -
With economy and election in their mind!
They are always there to guard it from all evils -
Like a mother of a newborn child!

Human brain needs a steady pure blood supply -
Even a computer requires a stable power supply!
But, the present and future of democratic free market people -
Depend only on uncertain, volatile and ambiguous stock market!!

Tax
(Dedicated to fair taxation reflecting physical labour distribution)

It is hard to imagine –
Once civilization evolved on Earth without 'Tax'!
When everyone worked as team together to serve and relax!
Lived as community sharing the fruits of productive hearts!
Enjoying festivities in freedom filled with creative arts!

Taxation started with the Warlords as they conquered!
Asked people to work and pay for their adventures!
Labourers paid for the Rulers without physical work!
Initiating inflation, ensuring future work is less worth!
Preparing the stage for politics of tax and 'tax cuts'!

Warlords grew in number harnessing military power!
Became King, Lord, Duke, Duchess, Knight and Maharajas!
Taxes and fees became part of the command structure!
Still ruling working class with democratic posture!
With never ending campaign of 'tough on crime' and tax cuts!

That is why the political campaign of 'tax cuts' -
Usually help people earning too much –
Without productive work!
Since we can't even think of modern life abolishing tax!
Let it be transparent value added tax –
On fair distribution of salary valuing real labour first -
Relieving citizens from the politics of inflation and 'tax cuts'!

God

(Dedicated to almighty eternal spirit)
From the very beginning of civilization -
Human wondered about natural evolution!
Fear of unknowns, mystic dynamism of creation
Overwhelming lights, sounds and visions -
Encouraged them to worship 'Blissful Energy' as God of salvation!

Humbled by eternal blessings and kindness -
They worshiped Sun as God along with Planets!
Romanticized by the power of universal forces -
They bowed with respect to spirits as natural causes!
'Hell' didn't exist making Heaven and Earth separated!

Everything changed since Alien invasion!
Humans saw Gods coming down in fashion!
Riding flying ships firing ammunitions!
Wearing suits and clothes beyond imaginations!
Triggering Historic Diaspora of human migration -
Installed Kingdoms ruling from urbanisation!

Most human died with new diseases and starvation -
Since world was not ready for hostile guests in millions!
Others enslaved to serve Priests, Archangels and Bishops -
Worshiped, sacrificed to please new heavenly illusions!
Priesthood, Sainthood stood guard as partisan -
Blocking mutual love and faith in God universal!

Abstractness grew between natural and spiritual world!
As priestly Kings ruled over everything on Earth!
Inventing Holy books erasing evolutionary past!
Claiming rules in scriptures are from Heavenly God!
Punishing all as blaspheme for disobeying new Lords!

Theories evolved on prophecies and miracles!
Religions formed and spread as institutions!
Prisons and jails became Hell on earth in millions!
Love for God, Faith in spirit, respect for nature disillusioned -
Frustration, disbelief, slavery, only led to fear for God!

One day, Jesus sat amidst people who listened to his words with amazement. He said:

"Seek not the Law in your scriptures, for the Law is life, whereas the scripture is dead. The Law is the living word of the living God to living prophets for living men. In everything that is life, is the Law written. You find it in the grass, in the trees, in the river, in the mountain, in the birds of heaven, in the fishes of the sea, but seek it chiefly in yourselves. God did not write the Law in books, but in your heart and in your spirit."

-- From the Gospel of the Essenes

Religion should be the ultimate testimony of truth whenever a society is built on some deliberate authoritative lies. This poem was written after extensive research* with an open mind to realize who Jesus really was which Bible has no intention to clear! Kolki)

From Jesus' Diary

My name is Jesus! Jesus of Nazareth!
Eesa, St. Issa, Apollonius, Budasaf, Yus Asaf!
I was born in ancient Palestinian City Bethlehem!
A true Semite uncircumcised not sent from Heaven!
No one told me the exact date -
But close to King Herod's end (5 or 6 B.C)
Certainly not the day you celebrate!

I realised in childhood -
God can't be violent only for good!
Can't protect some while destroy others
Must be 'loving and caring' to all in universe!

From Jesus' Diary (Cont.)

<u>Uncle</u> visited Jerusalem when I was a teen
Bringing Buddha's message to end all sufferings!
Spreading throughout east and far-east -
Embracing people beyond status and belief!
Mystified, curious, of <u>India</u> then 'Bharat',
<u>My maiden voyage</u> became following silk route!

Enchanted with eastern beauty, healing, hospitality,
Enlightened seeing peace achieved in universality!
Returned with joy to the valley –
Addressed my people oppressed, divided, inwardly -
Spoke for freedom we gain in love and mercy!

Preached against violence, anarchy and bigotry
How to live together as God's one big family!
Ignoring threats from heinous authority -
Carried out fasting for vision of blissful humanity!

Didn't want to die for Adam's sin voluntarily -
Rather wanted to live in peace having family!
Unaware how mean-violent head priest could be -
Pronounced God's name knowing its sin and <u>blasphemy</u>!
No matter how 'New Testament' spices it wasn't easy-
Carrying heavy cross on the top of the valley
Specially knowing it was meant for nailing me!

Tired, frightened, thirsty, running high fever
All I needed a bed, bread and drink from mother!
Instead received from some Jewish-Roman brothers -
Endless brutality, cruelty, one after another!

Knowing I taught against crusade -
They made cross holy after my death!
I spoke for freedom under God almighty
They censored Gospels strengthening their authority!
Rewrote scriptures claiming 'The Son of God'

From Jesus' Diary (Cont.)

Paid for all human sins dieing on cross!
Fulfilling prophecy as Bible taught!

Travelled a lot, surviving from cross
True Gospel my message and healing abroad!
In Syria, Turkey, Iran, India, Tibet -
Found respect, home, disciples among good friends!
Discovered in Kashmir lost Aramaic tribes –
Lived a long healthy life among peaceful followers
Finally rested in Srinagar 'The Heaven on Earth'!

Scriptures sent me to Heaven after resurrection
Placing me on Father's right hand, like a lazy son!
But my soul still hovers around earthly affection!
Whispers my message, can't be in sight –
Lest they label and kill this time as 'anti Christ'!

Wish list!
(Dedicated to the lost Heaven on Earth)

Friends! What I want?
Most of you don't even dare to ask -
Lest authority labels it as madness or terror!
If you had my wish list around
Communities, cities, countries, continents, emperors -
Would make a very different world!

God has given us everything
Still we ask for more and more, begging!
With doubts and fear of losing
Disposable knowledge, status, glory;
Belongings gathered in a cell of privacy!

Days, months, years, repeat again and again -
My humble wish list remains the same!
Buried under over industrialization
Untouchable in media of market orientation!

I want to be around
When human hymn the slogans -
'In a world full of grains, fruits, milk and honey
One hungry stomach is too many'!
'In a land filled with corporate space, estates and money
One homeless without a place is too many'!

I want to see a world
Where human are in high moral
Respecting their pray and exploits,
Without ever feeling in pride -
Its survival of the fittest!

I want to see the day
Humans coexisting same way
Animals and birds live in proximity
Without ever killing their kind any way!

Wish list! (Cont.)

When true religions evolve spiritually yet logically -
Universal God can only love all beings evenly!
Showering eternal blessings incessantly -
Never rewarding or punishing any form one-sidedly!

Mind enjoys happiness, soul feels rewarded -
Staying tuned to bliss-link despite earthly mandate!
Frustration, anxiety, disease, fear, bring despair -
Whenever greed, ego and anger make one blinded!

Satan has no meaning to God!
Evil prevails when a mind is blocked!
Satan and evil disappear
In the light of mercy and love!
I want to see Satan-less minds
Diminish evils with truth and trust
Facilitating return of 'The Lost Heaven on Earth'!
Now tell me, isn't it too much?

Poems by Kolki   About universal well being, peace and love   *Absolutely Humane*

Where is NATO now?
(Dedicated to end Palestinian sufferings due to ongoing Israeli aggressions)

[NATO's silence and inaction against Israeli aggressions and destructions in Lebanon and Palestine may cost NATO to be labeled as non-Semite Zionist Arm for world supremacy! It is time NATO sides with UN and <u>Jesus loving Christians</u> to order Israel to withdraw troops from Lebanon and Palestine and ask them to tear down the 21st Century Devil's Wall – The <u>Apartheid Wall</u> around <u>Palestine</u>. Kolki]

Where is NATO now?
I am a Lebanese Canadian –
Lost my wife and four children!
When Israeli military unleashed pre-emptive missiles -
Destroying apartment complex using US fighter jets!

Where is NATO now?
I am an UN Peace Keeper –
Lost my entire battalion!
When Israeli Air Force attacked our shelter -
Ignoring UN warnings and signs, threatening peace mission!

Where is NATO now?
I am a Palestinian parent -
Just lost my child!
When Israeli bullets -
Ripped through the brain, stomach and chest!

Where is NATO now?
I am a Palestinian child -
Just became orphan and homeless!
When Israeli missiles and US-made bulldozers -
Destroyed our home, belongings and assets!

Where is NATO now?
I am a Palestinian farmer -
Just became deceased!
When Israeli military tanks -
Drove over me while olive picking!

Where is NATO now? (Cont.)

Where is NATO now?
Palestine is still an occupied land -
After half a century of UN, US and NATO <u>diplomacy</u>!
Leaving peace loving Palestinians –
At the mercy of **non-Semite Zionist** <u>terrorism</u> for supremacy!

Where is NATO now?
We may not be of strategic Super Power interest -
Neither, we have vast oil reserve for the West!
Our freedom fighters are committed but not the best!
But, we are indigenous human suffering <u>High-Tech Holocaust</u> -
In our ancient land by Israeli military and political aggressors!

OIL

It's amazing!
How Arab world -
Providing most US and world energy needs
Be treated as enemy and terrorists?

It's amazing!
Why, Israel with no contribution to US
Be treated as ally
Receiving billions of US tax dollars unquestionably?

It's amazing!
How US politicians succumb to 'Zionist Jewish' lobby –
Despite Israel's violation of endless UN resolutions
Even destroying US navy ship during Egyptian war!
Killing hundreds of helpless US marines!

It's amazing!
America, with its wonderful friendly warm people
Helps breeding violence and terror in the world
Yet labelling its foreign policy victims as terrorists!

It's amazing!
Why American politicians and media
Doesn't look beyond CIA with self assessment
Converting speculated foes into real friends!

It's amazing!
How self censored gossip loving US media
Could shunt the best of US citizens
From worldwide love for peace and unity
And call for true democracy!!

National Security
(Dedicated to true security for the Human Race)

'National security'! Am I part of it?
I am one of the millions medically uninsured!
Out of census homeless!
Suffering from inflationary joblessness!
Prisoners whose voices blocked by thick wall cells!
Suffering from malnutrition as uninsured children!
Succumbed to surgery guarded by malpractice insurance!
Drink milk infected with injected hormones!
Eat meat full of chemicals and antibiotics unknown!
Work for minimum wage not enough for freedom!

I can be a statistics any day!
One of the millions dead from auto accidents!
Patient with AIDS, SAR or injury from police chase!
Heart attack eating fried food in fast food chains!
Gun related homicides or neighbourhood car race!
Soldier murdered in friendly fire as collateral damage!
Victim of genetically modified food on the shelf!
Ill-fated passenger of a flight terminated from cell!
Or just being in wrong time at the wrong place!

In a country of milk and honey -
I am one of the millions who go to bed hungry!
I am a good citizen, I love my nation!
I always played by the rules of the nobles!
Watched tax money reward billions for national interests!
Trillions in military budget remain unaccounted!
A few benefits immensely from a plundered 'Stock Market'!
When many like me suffer from basic necessity –
Of guaranteed food, shelter, education, job and medicine
How can they be part of the national security?

Birth Control Pills
(Dedicated to conscious healthy choice)

One pill a day –
A wife, a daughter must take
In anticipation –
That they might encounter sex
Conceiving untimely child unwanted!

Teenage girls –
With no desire for pre-marital sex
Or a grown up girl –
With no permanent boy friend
A wife who enjoys weekly or monthly once in bed
Must take a pill a day!

Breast cancer statistics increases every day–
As many encounter obesity helplessly!
Others busy removing unwanted hair growth desperately!
Still, ignoring dangerous labels on the vile
They know, must take a pill to satisfy!

Despite side effects and silent sufferings
Industry grows spending billions advertising
Politicians ignores worrying about jobs, instability,
Who could afford fighting against upcoming election money!

Media preaches the pill as a sign of freedom!
Man loves free sex without being responsible!
Sexual disease spreads, so does deadly 'AIDS'!
Commerce succeeds only women are enslaved!

Another Day –
(San Ramon, Pacific Bell Cafeteria (10AM), October 19, 1999)

Another Day in the San Francisco Bay Area
Another drive along Redwood Shores
Another look at the sleepy coastal range
Another fight with early morning Foster City traffic
Another commute over long San Mateo Bridge
Another struggle to pass through the town of Hayward
Another wait for the frustrating construction at Castro Valley
Another wonderful ride through the Crow Canyon Drive -
To San Ramon Valley, to Bishop Ranch, to work.

But today was different!
San Mateo Bridge had the same usual traffic -
Yet something was different!
The mystic fog over the water
Was probably right to make the rising sun
Appeared as an egg yoke
With a color of red hibiscus,
Floating on the glittering water!
Encouraging the birds
To fly in thousands forming patterns -
That lasted only momentarily
As the sun appeared brighter.

This was a special day!
An auspicious Hindu event, 'Vijoya-Dashami'
A time for sharing and unity
Bringing in hope for the millennium
With a message of co-existence with nature -
In a peaceful and meaningful world.

Just Being Black

(Dedicated to athlete Demetrius DuBose, 28, gunned down by San Diego Police in cold blood on July 26, 1999 and all victims of extra-judicial killings around the world)

Hi, I am (late) Demetrius DuBose!
It was summer of 1999 in San Diego!
The football season was just picking momentum!
I was spending time with my folks -
Before taking off for the Tampa Bay Buccaneers!

As I was leisurely driving down the Mission Beach -
It brought back many memories of good old days -
Including my play at the Notre Dame!

Suddenly, I saw flickering police lights from behind!
With high beam focused, urging me to stop by road side!

I looked at my odometer reading!
No! I was not speeding!
Is my license plate expired?
No, it is valid till next year!!
I stopped anyway and waited for the surprise.

Two police officers approached me!
And asked for my license and registration rudely!
I acted promptly, as I was enjoying favourite music merrily!

They ordered me to come out of the car!
'Anything wrong Officer?', I asked!

Come out of the car, 'mother F-word', 'Nigger'!
Or we will blow your head like a fire cracker!
Scared, slowly I stepped out of my car.

They ordered me to lie down with hands on my back!
As they were getting ready to hand cuff me -

Just Being Black (Cont.)

I asked again, 'Why? What did I do?'
'You can explain that to court', they yelled!

I was completely taken aback -
And didn't know what to do!
Then I got very angry as I felt insulted -
And urged them to let me go!

They drew their firearms pointing to me!
As I was shivering in a terrible fear breathing heavily!
Then I raised my hands extended forward
Urging them to hand cuff me politely -
While trying to explain who I was!

Suddenly, I heard two very loud booms!
And a quick feeling of missing body parts!
As blood was oozing out from my body!!
I tried to shout, but, couldn't say anything!
All I saw a rapid rewinding of my life events -
Ending in sleep at my mother's lap with pains!

Yes! Yes! Yes!
My brothers, sisters and citizens of the world –
I am Demetrius DuBose of Tampa Bay Buccaneers!
They killed me! They killed me in cold blood!
As if they were practicing shooting live objects.

They do it every day!
They do it in every city, throughout USA!
They did it because I was black!
They do it because we are black!
They do it because they know they can get by!
They cook many stories in media as they yawn!
But the truth is, they killed me -
Just because I was black!!

Free Market Oil
(Dedicated to all who suffer from the politics of oil)

They preach free market!
They dream global economy!
They sign international treaties!
For equality, rights and justice!
Except for oil, I mean crude oil!
Which must be cheap and cheaper!
To support industrial economy and military -
Making a few very rich fast and faster!

So, they divide Africa and Iraq!
Create Kuwait and middle-eastern dictators!
Calling them friends for National Security
While others, the supporter of free-market oil,
Suffer being labelled as terrorist and enemy,
Terrorized by mighty military machines
And their never ending sanctions and killings!

Thanks

Thanks to you all, my friends!
Thanks from the bottom of my heart!
Thanks for sharing your time for a noble cause!

It takes a voice –
A voice that is united, loud and clear
To maintain true peace and democracy
Threatened by a formidable super power!

It takes a village -
To raise and care for a child
Who will face this uncertain world!

It takes a heart –
A heart that's there to share
With the ones who need love and care!

Any great soul with a mission –
Is like a formidable mass revolution
Can accomplish all seemingly impossible!

Thanks to all noble souls
Trying to stand tall for truth and justice!
Crossing language and cultural barrier
Bringing back hope, peace, love and care!

Unity through Celebration!

The rhythm of Primitive drums, "Maadol",
Filling the air with festive mood – primeval!
Spreading the joyous message of celebration
Throughout the moonlit sky in vision!

Come, let us dance and sing along –
Before the clouds reappear covering the moon!
And let us resonate with the 'spirit of nature' -
Overpowering darkness and all evil fear!

Come; let us have a grand union –
Uniting every soul on this Earth!
And let us make our golden dream true -
Sharing the fruits of our united work -
In harvest, culture, knowledge, and freedom!

Maadol – An East Indian Tribal Drum

Without a President
(Dedicated to fare election and true democracy)

I don't have a president!
Yes, for next four years -
I am without a president.

I voted, as most American citizens did -
Electing State and Federal representatives!
But my vote for president went astray -
Without a simple complete, legitimate count!

My candidate was honest and candid -
Succumbed to age old rigging and fraud!
As George Bush, Jeff Bush, Katherine Harris
Planned a Florida wide minority vote blocked!

Knowing in advance minority poll -
Ballots got manipulated with confusing punched holes!
Just to re-assure big brother's hope -
Installed check points with scaring cops!

I like bi-partisan, I like action,
But how can I accept my president -
Without a fair election ??
Lost in popular vote and with less electorate -
How can one be president by the help of supreme court ?

So, until we count all votes -
To honour democratic world!
I will be without a president -
Alas!
ROME WASN'T BUILT IN DAY, SO IS USA!

Health
(Dedicated to healthy world)

'Health is wealth' is an old proverb!
Why people avoided disease being vegetarian!
Many eating Halal or Kosher!
Followed natural diet and practiced yogic posture!
Used herbs in cooking food as in Ayurveda!
Food therapy became household mantra in China!
Making nations happy, busy pursuing knowledge and culture!
Free from industrial pollution and burden of expensive health care!

Everything changed with inception of Roman Aristocrats!
Who ate and drank in party all night as elite!
Often vomited for further eating delight
Feasting on animal parts while still alive!

The aristocratic power marched on with crusades!
Invading Britain, France and Spain!
Installed Kings, Mercenary, Dukes and Knights
To Guard their fortune in the new world!
Inventing religion of cross replacing love of Jesus Christ!

Their craving for power, assets, resources, knew no bounds!
Soon they spread to America, Australia, and New Zealand!
Grew economy enslaving others destroying forest and ground!
Creating Industrial filths, military hazards,
green house gases abound!
Enshrouding Earth with endless fear from Bacteria and virus!

Food for thought is the mantra for good health!
Mind body connection helps one to rise above self!
Without good health life is nothing but burden -
Causing sufferings to neighbours, family and friends!

Snacks

When its time for snacks –
It is better to munch on grapes, donuts!
Carrot sticks, roasted unsalted peanuts,
Raw cashew, almond, pistachio nuts!

Hot Punjabi mix, nachos with cheese,
Fresh apple, sugar cane, pumpkin seeds!
Dates, fried eggplant, spicy potato treats!
French fries, samosa, roll, pakora, biscuits!

Goal-gappa, spicy puffed rice or chickpeas!
Coconut ball, falafel, peanuts with rice crisp!
Halwa*, chocolate, candies and cookies!
Cream crackers with Philly cheese –
Than carbonated drinks and potato chips!

*Halwa – Cream of wheat cooked with sugar and ghee;

Healthcare

[Author lived in Toronto, Ontario, for five (5) years before moving to New York. He lived in US for fourteen (14) years moving to Northern Virginia and eventually to San Francisco, California! Currently he has been residing in Victoria, BC, Canada, since January 2000]

Healthcare!
Yes, the Most Rationed US healthcare!
Where the premium increases every year!
As the high tech detection equipment flood the industry –
And healthcare dollars are invested in market economy!

The services get trimmed each year to maximize profit!
Limiting access to doctors and overall benefits!
Cutting down emergency hospital visits!
Forcing patients suffer silently without notice!

The cost of marketing increases –
Claiming the best health care system in advertisements!
Hiring top statisticians to exclude high-risk patients!
Lobbying politicians for their enthusiastic speeches!
Guarding status quo, "The market driven healthcare system"!

Void of the general well being and serving desires -
HMOs are minimizing hospital stay and emergency care!
Forcing even caring Corporations shop for the cost-effective plan
Making shareholders happy with additional returns!

The system works OK as long as premiums keep pouring in -
From contributors with no illness pre-existing!
With good physical and mental health state -
Leaving a third of the population without coverage!

The system makes one worry about the policy always!
Forces one to lose everything to care for the beloved!
Keeps young uninsured despite contributing for the elderly -
Discourages insured to use it less else pay premium hefty!

Healthcare (Cont.)

The system preaches the ill of 'National Healthcare'!
Spreads media lies undermining "Universal Care"!
Hiding true benefit of one plan managed by 'The People'!
Depriving free world enjoy good health in freedom!

Homeless

I am homeless!
I live on the city streets
And eat at the mercy of the passer's by.

I am homeless!
I have seen 60s, 70s, 80s,
Life is even tougher in 90s!
I see more of my colleague and friends on streets -
As technology advances at its best.

I am homeless!
I was in Vietnam War, I was in Korean War,
I was in desert storm, now disabled and out of work.

I am homeless!
I am a single mom, I am a single dad
I work at minimum wage and work between jobs
But still I am homeless.

My tax from minimum wage
Feeds a trillion dollar defence budget
Pays Billions for National Security
Leaving me homeless, hopeless and sad -
In a rich heartless developed world!

Peace now

[Let us remind the World Preaching <u>Domination is Terrorism</u>,
Acting to achieve it is <u>War Crime</u>! <u>Kolki</u>]

Peace now, peace now, peace right now -
No more war, no more war, no more aggression!

Peace now, peace now, peace right now -
No more bombs, no more missiles, no more occupation!

Truth now, truth now, truth right now
Collateral damages are death and destruction!

Peace now, peace now, peace right now
No more lies, no more pretexts, no more deception!

Truth now, truth now, truth right now
<u>We all know</u> who have weapons of mass destruction!

Peace now, peace now, peace right now
Peace is a direct threat to militarization!

Truth now, truth now, truth right now
Unilateralism could end civilization!

H1B VISA

They come to USA
As temporary business contract worker
Sponsored by –
Indian or American head hunters!

They gain American experience
Through on the job training
And get ready to change sponsor
As they gain confidence.

Soon they get pushed
By parents or fiancée left back home
To get married going back home?

They make their first trip
Back to India
Passage paid by the father of the bride
Get married arranged?
Totally by family and friends.

They come back to work in USA
Along with newly wed bride
Beautiful, educated, homey, smart and cultured
In an apartment surrounded by people
Totally unknown and foreign to her.

They become busy at work
Staying late to cover missed hours
During India visit and marriage efforts.

The new bride,
Can't work in USA
Without any honeymoon or site seeing,
Starts working at home totally alone
Cleaning and preparing food
For her arranged husband.

H1B VISA(Cont.)

Soon the bride, frustrated and lonely,
Tries to find friend
In a far way land
Getting involved in community events
Showing a little of her cultural strength!

Culture takes time
Away from home
Which gets obvious
Through rudeness and suspicion,
Quarrel and abuse
Worries and deception.

Finally, for family peace and security,
Surrendering to friends and in-laws
The bride gets pregnant!
Making everybody happy
Ending all worries for the groom and family!
And ensuring guaranteed US residence!

Village Path

(Translation from Nobel Laureate Rabindra Nath Tagore, 'Graam Chaara' in Bengali)

The unpaved village road of reddish soil
Makes my mind indifferent –
Reminds me of my link with the dust!

It calls me out of my home
To be part of the world of unknown!

It may lead me to materialism!
Entangling me with endless liabilities!
It may also help me receive -
The final message toward freedom!

New Born!

As we grow in life
And pass hurdles one after another –
We see the fruits of our efforts

Through rewards, appreciation and satisfactions
As degrees, trophies and accomplishments!

But none can parallel –
The birth of a child
Out of sheer love between a man and a woman
Feeling the power of creation
Hidden among complimentary human souls!

And what can be more satisfying
Than to hold the tiny hands
Of one's new creation
Watching him/her grow in baby steps –
As noises, giggles and screaming
Become language, laughter and expressions
When the very creation attains –
Manhood or womanhood!

Anniversary

Anniversary!
Comes in many ways –
Though it's all about celebration!

We celebrate birthday –
We celebrate graduation –
We celebrate New Years –
We celebrate holidays and religion –
We celebrate Independence Day –
We even create occasions to celebrate!

But, no celebration is like marriage anniversary!
Which comes every year –
As two separate souls
Come closer and closer
Trying to be one –
Assimilating all goodness of two
Solidifying the bond
Toward an everlasting unison!

Age Two

You are two!
It is nice to be two!
Two eyes
Two ears
Two eyebrows
Two nostrils
Two cheeks
Two lips, upper and lower
Two sets of teeth, upper and lower
Two hands
Two palms
Two elbows
Two wrists
Two legs
Two toes
Two knees

....

It takes two hands to clap
It takes two to make friendship
It takes two to share
Two means togetherness
Two can make a team

....

Two makes binary
Tow tides, high and low
Two poles, north and south
It takes two atoms to make a molecule
It takes two voices to form chorus
Two breaks loneliness
Two state of a switch, on and off
Two parent, mom and dad

....

There are many other reasons
To be proud of being two!
These are just a humble few......*Happy Birthday*

Happy Birthday

Birthday! An auspicious day!
Reminds the flow of time -
In every house in everyone's life!

The day comes following yearly cycle,
That's how people grow!
As children becomes young
And young becomes older,
Keeping the pace of life
Comes another birthday! An auspicious day!

Let it come with a new tune,
With a new message of the dawn,
As you (one) age(s) gracefully
Fulfilling the pursuit of love and knowledge!
Leading to happiness and prosperity!
Keeping the child inside ever alive
With the fruits of all past years!
Its your day and have a wonderful one –

(Translated from Deepak's Bengali Poem, 5/5/2000)

Cafeteria
(San Ramon, CA, written 11/22/1999, Pacific Bell Cafeteria)

Cash registers are officially closed!
They are now totalling day's transactions -
The cri-cridi-crik sound can be heard from a distannce!

Yes! Lunchtime is over!
In this huge yet artistic Pacific Bell main cafeteria!
Up stairs smaller cafeteria is still open
For the unfortunate ones who missed munching -
Attending outstanding work or unscheduled meeting.

Men and women down stairs
Are busy cleaning and packaging unsold items!
Loud sound of moving pots and pans on racks
Could be heard from a distance!

They are getting ready for tomorrow!
Some of them skipped their very untimely lunch -
Which is too early, 9:30 AM, around breakfast!
And now trying to eat something with lost appetite
Before rushing for the 4PM shift in another site!

The elderly lady ensuring salt and pepper in each table
For tomorrow's fresh start!
Bade goodnight to me with a very affectionate smile!
And some wonder in her bifocal eyes
About this very late sole customer
Sitting alone and writing in the huge cafeteria!

Beauty

Beauty, it's all around everywhere
Beauty, it's within in my mind!

Beauty, almost always makes be happy
Beauty, sometime also makes be cry!

My eyes are blessed watching beauty
Beauty almost always makes me high!

Morning brings me beauty of new creation
Moon light beauty really makes me sigh!

Dreams!

The song goes –
'Row, row, row your boat
Gently down the stream.
Merrily, merrily, merrily, merrily,
Life is but a dream.

Dreams are natural,
And seldom within our control!
Often, we call them sweet-
Sometime they become nightmares!

But, some people in free society
Can turn their dream into reality!
Owning your new home
Far away from your birth place
Is like a dream comes true -
Which you can cherish and nourish
As your own place in the world!
Congratulations!

Expectation

As we grow –
Our knowledge expands
Memory increases
Vision gets dimensions
Sense of responsibility grows
Try to be part of the society
Being integrated with its values
Getting used to imposed rules and regulations;
Religion puts additional barriers
Defining its own notion of the world!
News media make us attracted
To spicy and touching news
Politician uses the media
Shaping our political thoughts!
Commerce use the media
Dictating our needs and greed!
Scientists try hard to redefine truth
As Politicians and commerce hijack science!
Leaders urge us to have family values
While ignoring the very reason of disintegration!
Economists ask us to be a good consumer
Maintaining buying spree with debts!
Insurers want us to be covered
For the expenses incurred when I am in grave!

Stranger

Nature used to be everywhere!
Now they exist in National park or forest!
Nature is friendly to all –
We belonged to nature!

Animals used to be all over earth!
Now they can be found somewhere, in zoo!
Animals love you -
When they know you are not afraid or a threat!

Birds used to fill the land, ocean and sky!
Now most of them are in sanctuary or cage!
Birds can be friendly and funny –
To someone loving, caring and humane!

People used to be somewhere!
Now they are everywhere!
One can be friendly to people –
But many will ignore you as stranger
Some may convict you as alien!
And a few can shoot you as intruder!

Flying
(Written on Thai Airways, Oct 12, 1999, Tokyo -> Los Angeles)

Stretch –
Stretch your hands on the side parallel to the ground
Like the wings of the Canadian Geese!
Keep them stretched –
Until you feel movement of the wings!

Stretch your hands up -
As if you are reaching the sky
Keep them stretched –
Until you feel the lift!

Stretch your hands forward -
As if you are reaching the horizon
Keep them stretched –
Until you feel the takeoff!
Now close your eyes and think blank
Until you feel you are flying!

Free
(Dedicated to Dhruva the lovebird)

My lovebird, 'Dhruva'
Knows only one word 'Daddy'!
When he sees new things-
Or can't reason something!
Jumps on my shoulder sounding -
'Daddy, Kaeya Kaeya'!

He wakes me up in the morning!
As I brush my teeth, start shaving
Apply aftershave, cream, jelly
Put my shirt on, pull my pant
Slide the belt to tighten belly!
Dhruva tries his best to chant -
Daddy, Kaeya Kaeya!

As I take shower -
Use herbal shampoo, organic soap
Turn on the Jacuzzi full of bath foam
Use my towel to dry hair and skin
Dhruva keeps on repeating same thing –
Daddy, Kaeya Kaeya!

I brush my hair, comb eyebrows
Put on my lenses or eye glass
And steps on long corridor to reach bedroom
Dhruva makes few trips like jets without boom!
Glides and lands on my shoulder singing tune –
Daddy, Kaeya Kaeya!

I put my socks on then my shoes
Left hand holds briefcase right hand car keys!
I look for money bag, change, cell phone
As Dhruva shouts 'Daddy', reminding tea on stove!

Free (Cont.)

I start my car –
Look at the windows before changing gear!
Unrest Dhruva climbing the blinds without fear;
But his voice still ringing in my ears -
Daddy, Kaeya Kaeya!

Love

I wake up seeing your smiling face!
As I start free hand -
I look right, I see you
I look left, I see you
I look up, you are all over the sky
I look down, you are everywhere!
I close my eyes, you are within me!

When I smile, I see you smiling
When I appreciate something wonderful
I see your face wondered!
When I feel sad –
I see your face appears sad!

I meditate for world peace,
I feel your spirit resonant with me!

I sing my songs, I see your delighted face
I read my poems, I see my passion within you
I cook my favourite dish the way you like it!

I play some nostalgic music, I see your indifferent face
I look at my lively garden, I see your spontaneous smile
I look at night sky, your face is on each star and planet
I go to sleep, it feels you are just next to me
In my dreams, all I see is only you!

Hesitation -

I don't know what it is ?
Whenever I miss you too much
And my mind becomes very eager
To see you or just talk to you
I seemed to slow down
And hesitate to call you!

Doubts overshadow my feelings
Lest you don't appreciate my call!
Or I cannot express my true feelings
And may end up offending you!

As time goes by –
I feel even more hesitant and stiff
And feel stress from the notion of calling you.
Someone from inside asks me
To go for a long walk
To regain my thoughts and feelings!

As I come back from a long walk
I finally gain courage to call you
With my heart pounding
Each time the phone rings!

And then , suddenly, I hear your voice
Which I hear from within almost all the time
That sweet, simple, lovely and caring voice
Firm yet encouraging and affectionate
My soul gets very high
As if taking shower in the first rain
After a long drought summer.

Confession

Darling! It's a true confession!
I have no other intention
I know my limitation
But I love you!

I try not to think about you!
I do so many things just to forget you!
But all my efforts –
End up in deep longing for you!

I love your smile
I love your eyes
I love the way you talk
Just a mere thought of you
Gives me joy!

I try to be angry with you
Only to find my eyes wet!
I want to hate you
But a momentary sight of you takes me to heaven!
I don't know what to do
Besides telling I love you!

Jackpot
(Written in Dublin, California, when celebrating end of Golden Gate University courses, 12/16/1999)

Its party time –
People are drinking and shouting
In local bars and restaurants
Forming small groups
Maintaining simultaneous conversations
Without much meaning!

Its lottery time –
Lotto machines are cranking fast
Jackpot is in millions ($)!

Darling!
Nothing matters to me anymore –
As I am sitting alone
Looking at the mountain from the window
Just thinking about you –
Feeling you deep inside my heart
Saying to myself –
You are my jackpot and joy above all party!

Darkness

(Written in Calcutta, May 1997, when visiting for Father's illness)

It was dark!
I was standing on the concrete roof
After an electric power outage!

Everything quiet down
Except occasional voices here and there
And distant moving cars, buses or airplanes!

I looked at the sky –
It was full of stars and planets!
I saw Orion
I saw Seven Dwarf
I saw the North star
And the evening star!
I could even identify most solar planets!
I realized, I never looked at the sky
With such open mind before!

As I was staring at the distant stars -
In the deep dark sky
Noticing their flickering -
Suddenly I saw a shooting star
Just appeared and disappeared!
Painting your face
In the deep dark sky!
I saw a second one
Illuminating the last painting momentarily!

Hope

Just when I thought
I lost my love forever
As despair surrounded
Every moments of my life
When my dreams
Were full of disappointments
When love and commitment
Made no sense anymore
When I was afraid of dreaming anymore
You came back suddenly!
Without telling, 'why'
Without any fight or quarrel
Without any argument or complaint
You touched me silently –
And I saw hope again,
In your eyes!

Original

Darling (Baby!), my lady –
You are wasting your time.

Your eyes are beautiful
Without those external eyelashes!

Your lips are tempting
Without any lipstick!

Your hair is charming
Without a wig!

You look very feminine
Without silicone implants!

Your nails are blushing
Without any nail polish!

You look more human
Without the extensions!

You are natural and wonderful
Without most modern en-slaving tools!!

Beautiful

I could say my mother was beautiful!
She never had her hair made colourful!
Never used nail polish, lip stick or make up!
Never had to shave unwanted body hair!
Enjoying graceful eighties with normal wear and tear!

Now we hardly say with certainty one is beautiful!
Rather half heartedly exclaimed 'look beautiful'!
Because the apparent look may be deceitful!
Behind ornaments, garments and expensive decoration!

Women are born beautiful!
Until they are groomed into modern enslaving tools!
With make ups, hair style-colour, shaving and birth control pills!
Extended nails, false eye brows, wigs, implants and rouge!
People become doubtful whether someone is really beautiful!

Therapy

It's amazing –
That sometimes something so simple
Can contribute toward such great results!
Just a few pictures –
And recorded answering machine voices
Keeping me alive and giving me strength
To pass through the most difficult time of my life!

As I regain my strength
And look forward to new life -
I wish everyone else in this world
Enjoys similar feelings from a friend
Helping them to climb the mountain -
Of difficult time.

Winner
(Dedicated to Triana, a daughter never born, written 7/30/1999)

Darling! I never thought you would quit so easily
To make me a winner, in our loving competition!

It hurts so much to know you are so far away
Not just physically but mentally as well!

I loved you from my first sight of you
Then we took the vow to Court and God
That only death could take us apart!

You took me of guard when I was busy
To give you a new dimension in your life
Beyond just love and care!

You looked for new love to replace my old
Not knowing that my love was always new
And each day appeared newer to me
As long as you and your love were there!

I could easily rest a while
Being submerged in the pride of winning
But I will keep loving you even more –
Ensuring that you never can take me of guard again
This time, beating me in the game of love!

Imagination

That was it!
Just when I thought
I had everything -
A most fortunate man on earth
Life couldn't be better
Happiness is within my absolute reach
Luck and God were with me
All my hard work were worth
All my care touched her soul
All my love resonant with her heart!
Suddenly, I lost everything one by one!
Only to realize -
Nothing was there for me -
It was all my imagination!

Dilemma
(Dedicated to all who deserted me)

Honey!
I know you are ignoring me!
You stopped sending e-mail a day
Too busy to respond to mine always!
Phone rings cry -
Missing your sweet kind voice!
SMS messages feel the pain
Of remaining unacknowledged!
Your voice mail doesn't wait
For my longing voice!
Your distance and silence
Make me worry and impatient!
It feels like yesterday
When we talked for hours with eagerness!
You woke me up real late
Missing my call just for a day!
I can't explain staring at the sky
The reason you left everything behind!
I wonder are you well and happy -
May be tasting life with a new baby!
Just afraid to say good-bye
To once close loving humane buddy!

Deceiving
(Dedicated to all truthful hearts)

After a wonderful marriage of many years
When I was proud that we made it
Was ready to focus on my new endeavour
Working for general peace and happiness
Throughout the world!
My beloved told me -
She had been deceiving me!

She told me –
'You love me more than a human can realize,
Your love has no condition attached,
You enjoy loving me and caring for me,
But despite all I don't feel attracted any more'!

I told her –
'By deceiving someone one only deceives oneself!
I love you just as I love each breath
I miss you the way why planets revolve without rest
I can't even accept a small scratch in your face
I can't think someone hurting your rather childish self'!
So, baby, deceive me, tell me all lies,
But never leave me alone suffering separation!
Which will hurt my soul more than all deception!

Forget

Darling!
They ask me to forget you!
They want me to erase you
From my memory!

The Toyota Camry you bought -
Still parked in the driveway!
My gift Nissan Pulsar for your graduation -
Still looks new and reminds me of that day!

The house I am living in -
Is the same one -
You found after long search!
Your beloved Scandinavian leather sofa
Still makes guest homey and comfortable!

All the CDs we produced together
Are still in display on my piano!
Videos of shows we made together
Are labelled on the video shelf!

The keyboard you presented me on my birthday
Is now my best companion!
I still play the same harmonium -
You inherited from your mother!

The lovebirds you bought and cared for -
Are now my best friends!
They learned to call me daddy
As their children made me a grandpa!

You found new lover before leaving me!
But, as I am trying to make another fresh start -
Everything in and around me
Just reminds you more than ever!

Diwali – The Festival of Light
(Dedicated to an enlightened world bridging all barriers)

Let the light of 'Diwali' enlighten our mind!
To overcome all darkness in and around!
Bringing peace, harmony and prosperity abound!
Throughout this wonderful living planet of Sun!

It is the darkest night of the year!
This makes distant souls appear near!
Helps *communion with Saints or Dead* without fear!
Keeping in tune with Ramadan's fast and prayer!
Ignoring ugliness of Halloween terror!
Embracing each other in the spirit of 'Eid ul-Fitr'!
Let us kindle 'peace lights' uniting our beloved world!

Halloween

Halloween is 'all hallows E'en'!
Is the holy evening!
Day before all Saint's day
Celebrating Celtic New Year's Eve!
Christian Church celebrated popular feast
Until ninth century on May the thirteenth!
Became 'remembering the dead' on November 1st -
Coinciding with Celtic New Year Day at last!
Summer's end means celebration of good harvest!
Departed spirits return to visit kinsmen and guests!
Roaming around for warmth of good cheer!
Among good old family, neighbour and friends!
Celebrating 'All soul's day' and 'Day of the dead'!
Children collected food to feed the hungry and homeless!
Only commerce gains from Halloween's evilness!
Body decays, deforms, and decomposes after death!
But the soul always remains hallowed, bright afresh!

Cry
(Written, 12/7/1999, Redwood Shores, California)

Let me cry, please –
Don't ask me to take it easy!

Let me cry –
As long as my heart feels the pain!

Let me cry –
Until my mind is light again!

Let me cry –
Until my eyes are dry again!

Let me cry –
As my soul rises to a new consciousness
Makes my mind clearer than ever
And my heart gets ready
To love everything
In this living and loving planet!

Waiting for You
(Dedicated to Triana, a daughter never born, written 8/6/99)

I will be waiting for you -
As I surf television channels
Make breakfast in the morning
Cook your favourite dishes
Sing your favourite songs
Look at your smiling pictures
Remember you humming my songs
Recollect your childish voice
Dream your gentle and loving touch
Scold you for foolish mistakes
Eat at your favourite restaurants
Drive through your favourite route
Stop by the beach you loved most
Look at your disoriented clothing
Listen to your bold yet caring recorded voice
I will be waiting for you, baby!
With a broadened mind,
With wild romantic thoughts,
With a hope of your loving touch again,
When your loving voice will tell me -
That you love me!
That you need me!
And you are my baby!

Recovery

It's amazing to watch!
The same known person -
Who used to walk, run, swim and bike freely -
Learns to walk again following baby steps!
As she recovers from the terrible accident
Which split her left tibia and fibula!

It wasn't easy -
Bringing her back from abroad with a straight leg,
Making sure the pain is always little less,
Maintaining job, commute, school and home - alone,
Making sure natural food had enough calcium,
Ensuring proper treatment,
Facilitating every meal and drink within reach,
Yet, never letting her morale down -
Always with a positive smile !

Its really nice to see her walk again,
Sing and smile again,
Lessening all thoughtful worries –
Of true family and friends!

Real Love

(Dedicated to Triana, a daughter never born, written 8/31/1999, Redwood Shores, CA)

Its real love! Darling! Babe!
Its not affected by -
Your reckless driving
Totalling my car, ruining my insurance!
Yelling that you never loved me!
Undermining my native home and institution!
Irritation about my height and look!
Criticizing my songs and thin voice!
Disliking my hearty cooking!
Boy friends you collect on your way to nirvana!
Physical scars you left on by body and face!
Times you test my commitment and patience!
Leaving me sleepless alone!
Instigating pains for hiding the truth!

Because, the only thing that matters to me
Is I love you from day one
When I first met you
When I called you my wife at our first dance!!

Because I know that despite all your denial -
You loved me, you cared for me!
You waited for me everyday at the train station
With full faith that I will be there!
You taught me swimming and biking
Adding to my knowledge reading bed time stories !!

You cared for me when I was sick!
I cared for you when you were sick!
You protected me when I was in trouble!
I protected you when you were in trouble!
We had many adventures
Others can only dream of!

Real Love (Cont.)

Yes, sometimes I went overboard
Putting you into difficult situations! But
We sang together, we danced together,
We performed together, we produced together!
We solved difficult problems together
Working late through snowy cold nights!

We camped together, canoed together,
Even attended winter camping together!
We visited amusement parks together
Rode most rides in the world together!
We cooked together, we served together,
We had parties and fun together!
We drove together thousands of miles
Mostly through wilderness and wild beauty!

We biked together through parks and alleys
Playing hide and seek games!
We kissed each other, hugged each other,
Made love in many unusual places!
We taught together, we composed together,
We volunteered together for world's causes!

We prayed together, we worshiped together,
We argued together, we convinced together!
We recorded together, we published together,
We learned from each other, appreciated each other!

Honey! After all these togetherness,
You may keep saying that you never loved me
That you always hated my attitudes
And I would know that they are true
But I better keep on hearing those unpleasant-truth
Than living without you!

Baby, I love you, really love you, only you -

Real Love (Cont.)

And can't live without you, can't breath without you
Because you are blended in my mind
Because you are blended in my soul
You are always in my thought
How can I live without you -
Its real love. Always yours!.

Irreversible

Sun sets then rises again
Moon sets and rises again
Low tides spread the message of next high tides,
Clouds appear and disappear!

Sun is eternal orbiting our galaxy!
The moon keeps on revolving around the earth!
Water would remain in the ocean bed!
Droplets of water though in vapour state
Soon to be reunited as rain some day!

We often argue without reasoning
Leading to misunderstanding!
Misunderstanding can spoil relationship
Causing mental barrier!

Mental barrier may lead to logical blindness
Converting love to hate!
Hate can cause irreversible damage
To a person, society, country and the world!

Poems by Kolki About universal well being, peace and love *Absolutely Humane*

Funeral
(Dedicated to Triana, a daughter never born, written 7/29/1999)

Darling! It was so nice to hear from you
And feel your voice once more in my soul!

I am so relieved knowing you were having wonderful time
When I was going through nightmares
And all known relatives and my colleagues
Were praying for your safe return!

The letter from your lawyer never arrived -
Someone left a message for you from 'Action Court'
But never returned my phone call!

I was worried and felt like a dead man
Since your sudden disappearance
Wasn't the part of the plan you discussed
And we all had the worst fear
As you were staying alone in Grand Hotel
With your luggage, cash, jewellery and laptop!

I never stopped praying –
Just to know that you were safe and well
As I gathered all my strength
To bring you back, even from hell!

Now that you told me a part of your story
I won't bother you anymore!
But I will still love you as before –
Because love only teaches to give more and more!

Now I will be able to die in peace –
Knowing that my darling is happy
Getting what she always wanted to have
What I could never offer!

I know, I will never get the answer –

Funeral (Cont.)

How someone so known becomes so much distant!
But I will be happy knowing
That you are having a wonderful time
As they prepare my funeral!

Rejuvenate

Darling, you proved it again!
You can take my mind
To the highest point possible
And, at times, you can put me down under!
Just when I was feeling sad and was wondering
You came with a new look and spirit
And gave me an enormously joyous evening!
I was so happy to see you
Just like the way you used to be
Simple, beautiful, sincere and thoughtful yet humorous!
Soon, I got busy with my heap of work ahead -
But I noticed your smiling and sparking face
Again and again from a distance!

Return
(Dedicated to an united Bengal)

If I ever come back to this world
Whether by re-incarnation or resurrection
Or riding mystic science of evolution
Irrespective of Earth based religion
I wish I born again in Bengal!
A tiny ancient state, now divided into east and west
Embraced by tropic of cancer
North of Equator, a tropical paradise at its best!

Where soil is as fertile as in heaven
Gentle breeze carries fragrance of Eden
Flowers are charming arousing beautiful
Birds are plenty musical and playful
Songs find melody of the soil as <u>Baul</u>!

Where great rivers embrace the land
Ending their long journey in Bay of Bengal!
Fruits are endless in varieties and taste
Fishes are bountiful in ponds, rivers and lakes!
Vegetables look always lively seasonally fresh!
Multitudes of species crowd lush green forests!

Where animals are free as exotic as Bengal Tigers!
Boatmen and peasants are great philosophers!
Mountains end in the backdrop of the Himalayas!
Sandy beaches decorated with dunes, palms, casuarinas!
Festivities year round celebrate precious life together!

Where cooking is an art of creative herbs and spices!
Culture is blended in every soul that flourishes!
God is worshiped with devotional loving respect!
Meaning for stranger is unique, a special guest -
Cosmically known, part of Almighty beloved!

Saying of Kolki

[Friends, we all have to be busy to make a living. But when I got the opportunity after being a dedicated hard working slave to earn early freedom, I tried to be a listener of the universal messages buried under civilized noise staying alone and doing everything alone except growing my food. I wanted to share some of my general thoughts and realization which you may find appropriate at some point in life. Whatever we do to make a living in the industrial world we must always strive to search for truth, the main goal of our worldly adventure!]

Only love, mercy and mutual understanding can resolve problems we inherited created by many generations.

Once for all we must ask ourselves what made human the only animal who enjoys killing and destructing their own kind as well!

We all come to this world as listener, become reader, viewer, spectator, speaker as we grow up; but the wise always keeps on listening to be a knower!

One who claims awakened still sleeping, awakened one always feels awakening.

Truth is the basis of peaceful coexistence, without it efforts of achieving peace end in mindless gossips!

Anyone who is afraid of truth is a living dead who can be manipulated to harm own kind out of fear of bread!

Avoiding truth only widens the path of self destruction!

A conscious mind never gets angry but many enslaved ones see anger in truth!

What is good about liking peace if one doesn't act to maintain it!

Many people read what they like to hear! Wise read between lines to find what they don't hear!

Saying of <u>Kolki</u> (Cont.)

Wise speaks their mind not what other wants to hear!

Life itself as is positive, the only thing which makes it negative is excessive possession which we don't need but we burden ourselves.

When religion equates to power the violent ones spread faster!

Religion is science, becomes power and gossip when void of science!

When learned acts ignorant world becomes dangerous place.

Learned doesn't read news for research, their research become news.

Loving God leads to loving self; Fear for God leads to fear for self; Faith in God leads to faith in self; why loving God and having faith in God can bring out the best of human brain!

Religions on Earth may compete to claim whose God is Supreme, but labeling God as Supreme only separates God from everything!

Imagine if God as in Bible had only one son and human killed him for blood covenant being free to do anything without guilt including crusades against own kind.

Even blinds see God internally, others always seeing externally as well! But most often external vision blurs internal vision building a wall of separation.

Listening or reading is one thing but the joy of realization knows no bounds when comes from within.

Saying of <u>Kolki</u> (Cont.)

Caring leads to attachment. It is difficult to love and care yet stay detached.

Obstacles only help one to be creative if one can rise above fear from slavery.

Knowledge and love starts when a person plants a tree, sees it growing, and cares for it.

Knowledge is power, ignorance is fear; love is light, knowledge helps love spread without border.

Most human actions are spontaneous reactions in an effort to adjust with surroundings beyond control. Labeling only enforces status quo hindering natural evolution.

Controlling only postpones sufferings why one must let emotions flow to detoxify prior to realization – there is no short cut.

Once one utters God's name with love and affection, one hears the sweetest sound in the world.

One who cares for own children, family and community can feel God's pain for children dying around the world just for supremacy.

In a world full of grains, fruits, milk and honey - One hungry stomach is too many'!

In a land filled with corporate space, estates and money - One homeless without a place is too many'!

Peace is a threat to world wide private military industries and militia training trades!

Saying of __Kolki__ (Cont.)

Whenever National Security prevails over Individual Freedom a State is heading toward Military Transition!

Let us remind the World that preaching __Domination is Terrorism__, acting to achieve it is __War Crime__!

An economy based on defense industries, oil, real estate, logging, only leads to more infighting and overall destruction.

Forgetting is diversion but accepting in heart nothing lost makes sorrows or pain disappear!

It is the loneliness that helps human to realize they are not alone and never lonely!

While most suffers to embrace daily pain escaping freedom, some can use that pain to evolve from inertia of rest to inertia of motion feeling the power of human creation.

Expectation is natural. It is difficult to commit efforts without expectation. But often it diverts the determination needed to the reach goal of satisfaction!

Lovers share things spontaneously why they grow together without much worry.

Lovers don't need Valentine's Day, it's for people who forget to express love everyday.

In real love lovers feel each others missing and longing why planets move around the sun without getting lost in deep space separating!

Feeling of eternal love and bondage comes from mutual submission to each other shedding material ego while evolving with individual qualities to the fullest!

Saying of <u>Kolki</u> (Cont.)

Marriage is the most difficult decision in life for the learned! Getting married for them is the beginning of the problems, if not properly connected, mentally and physically! Others who marry for physical and biological need usually become happy bringing in children along with friends and family.

Detecting cancer is just the beginning of the bad news; everything else is down hill for the patient beyond all modern medical treatments, jargons and testing.

Cost of high tech detection is the main reason for sky rocketing medical cost as doctors ask patients to live with problems without much solutions than expensive surgical operations!

Electromagnetic modes or heat wave modes – Modes are always there its all about exciting them whether in heart beats, birth of a child, germination of a seed or application of waveguides – even implanting truth in otherwise indifferent people's mind.

One has to live life in a place to form proper views!

One can only teach oneself, it comes from within!

When one feels for plants and animals around, soon hears them and talks to them as company.

Imagine if God had to live with human adjectives or labeling by profession. Being vegetarian and pursuing knowledge with an open mind one can reach the Conscious State beyond one's profession, all acquired adjectives and religion.

Happiness is in one's mind. Some feels it in a crowded coffee house, some in temple others with family at home.

Saying of <u>Kolki</u> (Cont.)

Digging everything from earth faster for profit is alien mentality, natives always preserve with sensitivity.

Only fools talk about romance wise enjoy it!

Pure devotion helps one to be free of doubts and fear not possible just being wise!

Doubts and fear is the worst enemy of the human mind, knowledge and love is bliss which helps doubts and fear disappear.

Many dream and act to see a peaceful co-existing world which is presently full of nightmares!

Imagine if Buddha or Jesus had to worry about illness! Like animals and birds human can solve most health problems staying active, clean, eating healthy and avoiding stress!

Knowledge cannot console mind only love for the divine can.

Talking about love is one thing, realization comes from entire life.

Often learned creates perfect example where greed cannot see eternal kindness.

'Beauty really is in the eyes of the beholder'; what seems ugly to one can be charming to others.

No one knows when death comes, how! Why wise spends every moment to learn before saying good-bye!

Joy of reunion is overwhelming why universe evolves creating new stars and galaxies.

Saying of <u>Kolki</u> (Cont.)

Music is the language of the soul, writing, cooking and serving are the languages of the heart!

No one documented God's message like what Nobel Laureate Poet 'Rabindranath Tagore' did through his songs!

Cooking is the best human art which is also useful for body and mind.

Only tears can clear the path of realization! It doesn't mean pain but deep longing. What starts with pain ends in joy of union.

Wise give people gift as surprises, never give what other's want resembling trade.

One who can relish missing and longing during separation enjoys all fruits of union.

Tajmahal is beautiful so are many man made wonders but still inferior to an innocent smile or a little wild flower!

If one can maintain health eating tasty healthy food in less amount learning is wisdom.

Right height/weight is needed to keep disease away keeping in mind body needs 57% carbohydrates, 30% fat and 13% protein.

Losing weight shouldn't mean getting tired and miserable. A light vegetarian meal supplemented with nuts, fruits and milk, along with briskly walk or jogging can end most physical or mental sufferings!

It is better to munch on grapes, carrot sticks, roasted unsalted peanuts, raw cashew nuts, pistachio nuts, hot spicy

Saying of <u>Kolki</u> (Cont.)

Punjabi mix, nachos with cheese, fresh apple, sugar cane, pumpkin seeds, dates, fried eggplant or spicy potato treats, samosa, pakora, or spicy cheek peas, cookies, biscuits, cream crackers with cheese – **than carbonated drinks and potato chips!**

Body needs fat. If one doesn't eat enough body creates them and stores them. Body also creates fat whenever necessary to save organs from toxicity.

When two persons know their limitations and accept them they become good companions.

Only Slaves see sexual organs in human free ones see the divine in everyone why they only get physically aroused by their loving companion.

Sex keeps one young as long as one has self control and respect.

Love flows from self to family to community to country to world to God.

A child is the best gift human can ever receive reminding the momentum of continuity.

Human can do anything if they are free to try.

What is in a name? But there are names people can say million times only to feel enlightened!

Once one feels God by any name, the name becomes the sweetest and vision transparent.

A bad manager can make life on earth feels like hell, a good manager makes it feel heaven.

Saying of <u>Kolki</u> (Cont.)

A man feels great being a dad, a few feel the greatness of being universal dad.

Once people start complaining about their natural season soon they become out of tune from nature's protection!

Often crying means sufferings but learned can steer them to feel the joy of new meaning.

We will have happiest day and saddest day in life. But sometime one event may give us same feeling inside.

We must be digging to make a better living bearing in mind a safe easy return to top before leaving!

A good composer writes in the brain when working, walking, serving or gardening before documenting feelings through music or pen!

We are born world citizens to discover some communities, cities, countries, religion treat us as alien!

God once blessed human giving them a brand new world, pristine environment, hospitable Native people and sages with cosmic wisdom!

War-Like
(Dedicated to all who suffer from civilized terror)
[In the age of High Technology, do we need the World War II sound of terror in Police Cars, Ambulances and Fire Trucks? Kolki]

From dawn to dusk, night to morning -
Ambulances passing through city streets speeding!
Police cars racing with emergency lights flashing!
Fire trucks rolling through neighbourhood screaming!
Horrifying animals, children, patients with unwanted warnings
—
Reminding aged constantly their time is nearing -
War-like sirens and scare just normal daily living!

Corporate managers busy running war rooms -
Brainstorming survivability in global rules!
Employees must take their best shots at the new bull -
Staying on call with beepers, cell phones, being mindful!
Fearing competition, job security for family and breads -
Stress is normal like a doctor by the emergency bed!

Presidents-Prime Ministers get briefings of intelligence -
Which country is advancing beating analysts estimates!
Downsizing, outsourcing, subsidies to trades -
Blame the peacemakers knowing peace is a threat!
Identify leaders gaining stability in economic strength -
Justify more military spending for national interests!

People at bars and clubs, looking for a smoking gun!
Children's book to video game killing is just another fun!
In news, movies, television, gossips and theatres -
Crime is dominant so is suspicion of terror!
Homeland security, Air Marshals, Internet Fire Walls -
Bird Flu, SAR, Mad Cow Disease, War on Terror -
Normal life in our World is just readiness for another war!

Poems by Kolki   About universal well being, peace and love   *Absolutely Humane*

New Pearl Harbour
(Dedicated to all who have been suffering the wrath of world supremacy since 9/11)

NEOCONS in the United States of America had fantasy!
To rule the world in peace time with hostile vision of Supremacy!
Where, as minority, they govern US and the world with secrecy;
Maintaining parallel military Government hijacking democracy;
Installing NEOCON ambassadors in UN and Embassies!
Indulging citizens in gossips and rumours of private ideology!
Spreading Al-virus in the cyberspace exploiting technology;
Occupy promise world fulfilling Biblical Prophecy!

So, they wrote in peace-time the dossier of world supremacy!
'PNAC', The Project of the New American Century!
Reviving century old imperial tools of divide and rule policy!
Dismantling all peace initiatives, poisoning global intimacy!
Financing NGOs as crusaders –
For the International Republican Party!
Asked then President Clinton to sign and implement it!

Rebuffed from a man of passion and extreme humanity!
They trapped his vulnerability –
Using Jewish American Monica Lewinsky!
Ruined the possibility of Al Gore Presidency –
With constant publicity!
Marred 2000 election with deceptions and fraudulent activities!
Patronized cunning George Bush for presidential candidacy!
Encouraged Supreme Court for undemocratic Republican victory!

With firm grip on NSA, CIA, FBI, NASA, FED and Military –
They fooled Clinton Administration with false Al-Qaeda activities!
Framing Islamic militants –
With tips from German Intelligence Agency!
Revived idea of Military Coup –
Rebuffed in sixties by President Kennedy!
Started implementing 'New Pearl Harbour' –
Under George Bush's presidency!

New Pearl Harbour

The military plan of hijacking Passenger Jet –
Came to life from infancy!
Hiring Dov Zakheim, the Guru in Flight termination technology!
With knowledge of 'Home-Run' –
Locking Boeing 757/767 as drones remotely!
All they needed –
Change existing NORAD fighter scrambling methodology!
Making Mike Canavan of Federal Aviation Administration
The sole contact using presidential authority!
Transferring WTC ownership to private from Port Authority!
Implementing demolition plan –
Under well guarded FBI and Mayoral authority!
Rescheduled 'Global Guardian' –
Before Colin Powel's UN diplomacy!
9/11, **a bolt from the blue**, -
Empowered NECONS with dream publicity!
For unleashing 'Shock & Awe' –
The ultimate terror, destruction and hostility!

9/11 Hijacking

(Dedicated to all who have been suffering for well coordinated 9/11 disaster)

[How Western Media and Politicians betraying Citizens without addressing trivial 9-11 anomalies! Kolki]

[NEADS – North Eastern Air Defense, FAA – Federal Aviation Authority]

If Bin Laden had to mastermind 9/11 operation
First he had to change normal US-hijacking protocol!
Overriding NEADS sector commander's power
Of scrambling fighter jets after the hijackers!

If Bin Laden had to execute 9/11 disaster
He had to authorize Mike Canavan,
As FAA hijack coordinator,
The sole contact for the National Military Command Center
And making sure he hides in Puerto Rico without answer!

If Bin Laden had to coordinate 9/11 as commander
He had to order **General Montague Winfield Brigadier Entrust** Charles Leidig, the deputy for Command Center
In charge overseeing the period during disaster!

If Bin Laden disciples were the hijackers
They would have been listed as passengers!
With their Islamic names on ticket and computer
Validated by passport and licence having picture!

If Cessna trained hijackers somehow could hijack
Pilot or crew had ample time to activate transponder!

9/11 Hijacking

Located at multiple points throughout jet airliners
Informing ground control 'I have been hijacked'!

If box cutters armed hijackers could over power
All captains and crew members, taller and stronger!
The takeover saga would have been there
In cockpit voice recorder for half an hour!

If Cessna trained hijackers could fly Boeing jetliners
Flight turns would be at the mercy of Boeing flight software
Having built in restriction maximum 1.5g manoeuvre
Could never collide with WTC –
Overriding anti-collision feature!

If Bin Laden and hijackers with box cutters
Could undertake such mission of precision mass murder
President Bush must have ordered 'Global Guardian'
Bring those drones down locking on transponders!

Poems by Kolki   About universal well being, peace and love   *Absolutely Humane*

Daniel Pearl

(Dedicated to all true fearless Journalists around the world)

[World must not forget non-Semite Zionist dream is not just Palestine, it is the covenant with their God to rule the Promise World. Kolki]

[ISAYAH 2:2 - It will come to pass IN THE LAST DAYS, *that* the mountain; *promotion,* of THE HOUSE OF YAHWEH WILL BE ESTABLISHED IN THE CHIEF OF THE NATIONS, and will be raised above all congregations; and all nations will *eventually* flow to it]

Daniel Pearl went to Heaven after death!
Kidnapped from Pakistan, murdered in secret!
While investigating Al Qaeda-ISI links Richard Reid of Britain!
Tracing $100,000 wired to 9/11's alleged dead chieftain -
Mohammed Atta's US account by Ahmad Omar Saeed,
Instructed by General Ahmad Mehmoud of Pakistani Intelligence!

God waved at him addressing 'Hello my son'!
Let me first congratulate you for what you have done!
Even I would have thought twice for such daring ambition!
To unfold Super Power consipracy of occupying new world!

Enjoy Heaven, rest a while before time for resurrection!
Don't endanger life running around the world for information!
Roam around in disguise only in and around Washington!
'Al' virus spreaded Uncle Sam converting America Zion!
While Bin Laden fights against US's Arabic mission!

I blessed US once giving pilgrims an wonderful land!
I blessed them again with hospitable Native Americans!
I blessed once more making leader like George Washington!
Hoping they live free respecting all in an unspoilt dream world!

Daniel Pearl (Cont.)

But they commited sins <u>killing innocent Native Americans</u>!
Then transfering hard won people's power to <u>private hands</u>!
<u>Defense industry</u> fulcrum of 'Axis Power' rest around Pentagon!
Why I am sending you back again with heavenly protection
To expose <u>supremacy truth</u> radiating from <u>Washington</u>!

Neo-<u>Nazi</u> is way past!
But <u>Neo-Con</u>/<u>IRI</u> clear and present danger!
When alleged <u>9/11 plotters</u> –
Running US Administration's <u>War-of-Terror</u>!

Poems by Kolki   About universal well being, peace and love   *Absolutely Humane*

Inconvenient Truth

(Dedicated to a truthful society where law makers, leaders,
intelligence and military can speak <u>truth</u> under oath)
[Ever wonder why a <u>sect</u> of Earthly Human would strive to achieve promise
land in a new world that God created for all? <u>Kolki</u>]

World Leaders know from <u>intelligence</u>, during <u>9/11 disaster</u> -
<u>NEOCONS</u> executed the <u>worst crime</u> against the Americans!
<u>Masterminded</u> in the White house –
<u>Implemented</u> from the Pentagon!
While <u>framing</u> and <u>blaming</u> Bin-laden and Islam!
Terrorizing citizens -
With planned massive <u>propaganda for War</u>!
Silencing Lawmakers and News Anchors –
With the threat of <u>Anthrax</u> virus!
Enshrouding America with a secret <u>virtual fear</u> from far,
Bringing to light Founding Father's worst <u>nightmare</u>!
So what? Hush-hush, whoosh-whoosh!
They are the <u>chosen to lead</u> the world after all!

Day before 9/11 -
Defense Secretary <u>Donald Rumsfeld</u> –
Had a press conference!
Disclosing <u>Pentagon's inability to track $2.3 trillion</u>
In dollars and cents!
<u>9/11 disaster</u> and terror –
Buried all investigations and media attention -
Facilitating funding for Vice President Cheney's
Secret <u>Monarchist</u> mission!
Of governing USA <u>bypassing accountability</u> –
With <u>personnel invisible</u> ready for global actions!

Inconvenient Truth (Cont.)

Building the basis of 21st Century <u>world wide crusades</u> -
With <u>terror</u> in vision!
So what? Hush-hush, whoosh-whoosh!
Chosen needs <u>Constitutional Monarchy</u> -
For crusades off and on!

After 2000 US election –
World was speechless watching US Presidential <u>voting fraud</u>!
When <u>Judges ruled to stop vote counts</u> electing <u>NEOCONS</u>!
Slapping American rights, free speech and freedom!
Resurrecting militarism, ending civilized conflict resolutions!
So what? Hush-hush, whoosh-whoosh!
It's the ancient <u>Israeli practice</u> after all!

World War II was over;
Germans surrendered, Japanese disoriented!
<u>Manhattan Project</u> resulted in <u>Atom Bombs</u> newly tested!
Scientists, humanists, politicians –
<u>Rallied against</u> atomic weapon deadliest!
But all they needed –
<u>Einstein's</u> blessings for military clearance!
That <u>destroyed Hiroshima and Nagasaki</u> within moments!
So what? Hush-hush, whoosh-whoosh!
Chosen's actions are always prescription for <u>annihilation</u>!

Egyptian War, 6-Day War, was ravaging Middle East!
<u>USS Liberty</u> observer ship was patrolling for peace!
<u>Israeli Air Force pounded Americans</u> with missiles at ease!

Inconvenient Truth (Cont.)

Killing 34 soldiers, wounding 171 –
Unarmed waving American flag at sea!
But the truth never reached the Americans for allied secrecy!
So what? Hush-hush, whoosh-whoosh!
<u>Friendly fire</u> and deceptions are always Chosen's strategy!

Throughout history –
<u>Assassination</u> is their strategy blaming patsy!
<u>Killed Hebrews</u>, Buddhists, Hindus, Christians, Moslems…
without mercy!
Started World Wars in disguise <u>hijacking Nazi</u> Party!
Why United Nations <u>banned</u> them as the most racist entity!
But nothing could stop them –
From <u>hijacking</u> American Democracy!
So what? Hush-hush, whoosh-whoosh!
They need to ride on Super Power –
To fulfill Old Testament <u>Prophecy</u>!

World was ready for <u>peace</u> –
Resolving conflicts and implementing <u>global initiatives</u>!
<u>Signing Kyoto</u>, defining <u>Palestine</u>, banning <u>deadly mines</u>!
Embracing once for all –
'Blessed are the <u>peacemakers</u>' slogan!
So what? Hush-hush, whoosh-whoosh!
Peace is a <u>threat</u> to <u>chosen's</u> hold of their Promise <u>World</u>!

Without 9/11
(Dedicated to a truthful world and all suffering souls due to mysterious 9/11 without open public investigation)

Without 9/11 –
Thousands of Americans still be alive on Earth with vigour!
Hundreds of fire fighters would be rescuing with honour!
World trade center would be standing tall in New York!
US taxpayers would enjoy trillion dollars for homeland care!
Defence industry would starve from 40 billion terrorism fear!
Kyoto will be ratified and implemented with cheers!
Land mines would be banned as true evil in civilized world!
US administration won't be nightmare of Founding Fathers!

Without 9/11 –
Al-Qaeda would never exist virtually!
Taliban would run Afghanistan as citizens lawfully!
Bin Laden would be seen preaching physically!
Iraqis would still be enjoying sovereignty peacefully!
Airport security won't harass people with delays and worries!
US/NATO/Israeli war crimes couldn't hide under insurgency!
Terrorism wouldn't seize most national agenda in 21st century!

Without 9/11 –
Suicide bombing won't be an industry of the military!
Anthrax perpetrators would be in jail not running country!
World won't be scratching heads for endless anomalies –
Why Holocaust survivors so united for war with secrecy!
Neo-Conservatism couldn't hijack main stream Conservatives!
Most media won't be plagued with patriotic nationalism!

Without 9/11 – there is no 'War on Terror'!
World would have redefined war as the vehicle of Terror!
Earth would have been better with message to share and care!
Establishing unity with equity –
Ensuring freedom beyond borders!

Poems by Kolki   About universal well being, peace and love   *Absolutely Humane*

Terrorism
(Dedicated to all who suffer from real terrorism)

[For the sake of humanity all UN members, Scientists, Engineers, Lawyers, Politicians, Academics, Doctors, Philanthropists, Journalists and Trade Unionists must stand together and ask for open public inquiry ensuring whether nameless novice hijackers with box cutters can cause massive <u>9/11 disaster</u> evading NORAD, CIA, FBI and US military! Also whether a truck full of Ammonium Nitrate can cause <u>Oklahoma City Bombing</u> Damaging FBI building! World cannot afford a Super Power being run my <u>Criminal Administration</u>, Intelligence and Military in the 21st Century! We must find the <u>truth</u> once for ever for the sake of this world! <u>Kolki</u>]

Terrorism lets <u>NASA hit comets</u> without universal consent!
Militarizes space for pre-emptive strikes as <u>missile defence</u>!
Makes heroes out of people who are free to kill with licence!
Empowers scientists to build Weapons to destroy citizens!
Motivates leaders to mastermind <u>illegal wars</u> in secret!
Instigates chosen groups to treat others as <u>slaves</u>!

Harmonizes World Health Organization to spread bio terror!
Synchronizing with military invasion –
Of self proclaimed Super Power!
Ensures commons besieged with pandemic rumours!
Diverting military atrocities and abuses with a cover!
Motivates technologists develop sterilized seeds for the growers!
Encourages law makers to break laws casually with humour!

Urges human to enslave others to reach honourable position!
Emboldens pimps hunt for children to run prostitution!
Blocks learned brains with greed of short term temptation!
Lets citizens in need suffer most –
From irresponsible manipulations!
Insensitizes heart –
Preaching hunting as a game not assassination!
Creates <u>NGOs</u> –
To subvert true democracies as United Nations!

Terrorism

It hides behind intelligence and national security mask!
Asks people to settle for less as countries advance!
Destroys natural stimulants for selling synthetic drugs!
Excites politicians to justify delay in retirement perks!
Lets decision makers succumb to military desires -
As they suffer from secret pain of undisclosed massacres!
Empowers managers to fire honest and hard workers -
Persuades Law keepers to silence witness with violent gestures!
Overpowers brain with evil dominant desires!
Blinds judgement of consciousness to ignore war criminals!

It mutates staging Jerusalem fire or 'New Pear Harbour'!
Gaining momentum with deadly technology and media takeovers!
Since it inspired Hebrew G-d to invade Canaan to occupy Earth!
Baptised Constantine to embrace cross instead of Jesus Christ!
Motivated Pope Urban II organize crusades in the name of God!
But could never survive –
The light of united hearts seeking truth and love!

Delegation
(Dedicated to all world citizens)
[If you ever feel compelled to write and campaign for peace, remember many around the world share your views and will find reasons to make it news. Kolki]

Friends and world citizens!
There comes a time for change!
Some seize it others try to sleep well!
Many ignores after working hard for bread!
Submerge minds in light entertainment!
Worries about job, security, never end!
Why momentary pleasures reminds of Eden!
Reality enshrouds the moment illusion ends!
Good intentions get lost in gossips, inert quarrel!
Truth is the only weapon for a peaceful end!
Lies and rumours hunt easy pray to sustain!
Isolation and humiliations frustrate thoughtful brains!
But never forget 'Where there is a will there is a way'!
To accomplish mission just be the change!

Expression

The first expression is always hard!
Whether writing a letter, poetry or in love!
Even most famous writers found it difficult -
To send the first article with doubts of repercussion!
Epoch poets stumbled for the beginning line!
Even actor, actress, hero, heroines -
Had to work hard overcoming shyness first time!

Interest groups formed all over!
Dividing humans –
As liberals, conservatives, gays, lesbians!
Reviving 'Us versus They' slogans!
Let us express ourselves without rehearsals -
Before we reach point of no return –
From backward evolution in history forever!

Poems by Kolki   About universal well being, peace and love   *Absolutely Humane*

21st Century Stake
(Dedicated to worldwide transition to a truthful and just society)

[Some imperialist leaders scare citizens about 21st Century stake! Many allied leaders get easily baptised with the gravity of the stake; but all of them underestimate their democratic citizens with a veil of secrecy guarding the agenda of few chosen who have been playing this stake-card since Biblical events. <u>World Wars</u> were fought to suppress rise of the people toward formation of an <u>egalitarian</u> society!   <u>Kolki</u>]

21st century envisioned a chance to learn from mistakes!
Urging people to act implementing a global village!
Reinforcing rule of law forming <u>International legal offices</u>!
Ratifying <u>KYOTO</u>, <u>banning weapons</u> that kill masses!
Opening up countries with free trades for goods and services!

But these worldwide united efforts made few <u>chosen</u> afraid!
They know well, world peace and unity is against their lineage!
Without divisions and wars they will be like everybody else!
Nobody would honour them as God sent to rule the slaves!

Why few educated chosen wrote <u>supremacy dossier</u>!
That openly terrorises the world –
Using military, <u>NGO</u>s and cyberspace!
Justifying war time spending in peace time –
For <u>Rebuilding America's Defenses</u>!
Creating '<u>New Pearl Harbour</u>' –
To unleash unquestionable dominance!

The stake is good news for Indigenous growth to the fullest!
Without domination, slavery or hegemony from crusades!
Bringing back pristine world of truth for festive co-existence!
Enjoying heavenly peace together <u>not a military threat</u>!

Just the way ancient Jews-Amorites lived in Semitic co-existence!
Celebrating life attending Churches and Temples!
Praying for peace, prosperity, with neighbourly gospels!

21st Century Stake (Cont.)

Undivided where strangers were wise men not aliens!

But Hebrew God was <u>afraid of strangers</u> from the East!
Needed kings and nations for the <u>new circumcised</u> to lead!
Why '<u>House of YEHWEH</u>' preparing toward doomsday,
Anxiously waiting for their role in <u>Armageddon</u> to play!

Their fear is that the commons are being united -
In <u>Temples</u>, <u>Mosques</u>, <u>Synagogues</u>, and <u>Churches</u>!
Singing for freedom from few dominating forces -
Welcoming transition to regain lost faith and openness!
Bringing back heaven on earth for peaceful coexistence!

Pests

We build home on the ground -
Kill cockroaches, snails, slugs, mice as pests!
We log forest make farm lands -
Rabbits, deer, gypsy moths, birds become pests!
We destroy wilderness for farm animals -
Bears, wolfs, mountain lions are new pests!
We fish with trawlers sweeping ocean bed -
Seagulls, pelicans, sharks are beachside pests!
We form cities housing millions -
Open ground rats, crows are now scavenger pests!
People move to suburbs, build fenced yards -
Grazing deer, racoons become neighbourhood pests!
People find new continent with pristine nature -
Survive with food and drinks in native shelter -
Enjoy honest hospitality and free culture -
Only to treat natives as pests in convenient future!

Homey
(Dedicated to freedom and justice for all sentient beings)

World used to be their home in freedom!
Before human claimed and partitioned land!
The mountains, valleys, meadows, woods -
The pot holes, ponds, lakes and bogs,
Were all accessible for food and fun!

Before they realize the human face!
Their freedom of movements got curtailed!
Grazing lands became partitioned, divided -
Guarded with cruel obstructing fence!

They are the deer a symbol of peace!
Try fruitlessly to hide and graze at risk!
Whatever grassy yards still left unfenced!

Some adores them, others hate them as pests!
Many want to kill to save dear garden!
Others want to hunt for a rare gourmet!

It's autumn, leaves are falling everywhere!
Views around are getting brighter and better!
My yard is unfenced, blended with nature!
Where my lovebirds feel free, so are the deer!
As they rest with babies without fear
Grazing and grinding merrily
Feeling at home and making my home homey!

Heir
(Dedicated to future generations)

What kind of world we are leaving behind -
For our children and future generations?
Pay interests on debts incurred by our short sighted vision?
Drink toxic water from our greedy pollution!
Breathe air full of filth of industrialization!
Suffer uncertainties of global warming devastation!
Be 'Tough on Crime' ignoring irresponsible distribution!
Accept militaristic civilization as democratic <u>illusion</u>!
Ignore perils from domestic weapons of mass destruction!
Fight '<u>War on terror</u>' chasing virtual Boogeyman in action?

Live in private cells singing 'Don't worry be happy?'
Believing Superman will fight evils of Anarchy -
Santa Claus prevails as global Toy Industry!
That Dooms Day will succeed over all human <u>diplomacy</u> -
Proving covenant of supremacy is eternal not just prophecy?

Mean
(Dedicated to a caring world)

After a long and exhaustive search
For Krishna my dearest lovebird
Through nearby neighbourhood and forest
Half-hearted mind wanted another ad
In local newspaper under citywide classified!

The phone rang in the evening
As I was having dinner after hard work
Tired thinking what really happened to her
Eagerly answered the precious caller!

Couldn't believe the message at first
An elderly voice saying they have my lovebird!
Only to let me down in despair
Saying 'she is wonderful for making love'!

I hung up with thanks for the call
Wondered how mean can be some human!
Even age couldn't turn them as the best animal!
Like many media blogs and talk shows become popular
Cheering viewers with casual jokes about disasters
Often with personal attacks on politicians and leaders!

Dead End
(Dedicated to old is gold)

When senior citizens talk like the beginners!
Discussing interests, stocks, funds, like profiteers!
How to grow money fast and faster!
Watching talk shows, golf, boxing, pornographic materials!
Preaching economic benefits of wars!
Sending chain mails for fortune or kindness from billionaires!
Scaring people with rumour of unknown racist fear!
Believing in a few rip their wallets staying out of work!
They reached the dead end before they disappear!

Couldn't see the path of enlightenment staring on sides!
Misused the knowledge learned throughout life!
Couldn't see the hands extended for friendship around!
Didn't hear the call for the journey ahead to new world!

Renounce

(Dedicated to all enlightened souls)

We all appreciate great souls!
Read and adore their achievements
How they renounced life as is
Searching for truth and enlightenment!

We tell stories to children
Glorifying their work with miracles
Achievements seemingly unachievable!

But when one of us
Dear family or friend
Tries to do the same
We get scared, bewildered!
Search for Doctor's immediate help -
Equating would be great noble –
Unsociable, abnormal, **schizophrenic menace!**

Palestine

(Dedicated to the modern State of Palestine and all martyrs, written April 20, 2006)

Palestine O Palestine!
Reminiscence of the ancient time!
The first recorded civilization of human kind
Once prosperous City-States of creative mind!

Linking ancient Egypt, Mesopotamia and Assyria
Your culture and goods reached ancient China and India!
A free land with high spirit known in history as Canaan
Vibrant small communities –
Celebrated life by the Mediterranean!

Your peaceful festive society and culture
Ended with Hebrew God's worldly adventure!
As invaders burned your civilization with deadly massacre!
Ending thriving natural life style in nightmare!

You witnessed wars, occupations, annihilation in repetition
Bloodshed and revenge –
Covered once pure land with pollution!
Influx of people found home surviving migratory persecution
Some destroyed you –
While others blended in cultural unification!

Your modern democracy was destroyed at inception
As the powerful evil force besieged you with obsession!
But you rose again from the ashes of oppression
As an inspiration to the dream of worldwide freedom!

Silent cry
(Dedicated to worldwide sustainable consciousness)

Whenever insects are crawling around suburban homes -
They are crying for help lost their place once they own!

Whenever campuses by Farmlands are overwhelmed with bugs!
They are crying for help scared from pesticides attack!

Whenever seagulls are crowding ocean beach screaming!
They are crying for help their food is victim of deep sea trawling!

Whenever people are sleeping by the street or begging!
They are crying for help untouchable in a feudalistic economy!

Whenever wars being fought for aggression with media posture!
Victims are crying afar from death, destruction, abuse and torture!

Whenever engines are running, objects are roaring through sky!
Noise erupting from construction, mining, or explosive device!
Molecules are crying for help from mechanical pain out of sight!

Whenever earthquakes devastating civilization like strokes!
Tornados, Cyclones, sweeping surface in destructive mode!
Volcanoes erupting –
Vomiting ashes in the sky spreading lava remote!
Mother Earth is crying in pain –
From endless logging, digging, killings and noise for material gain!

Poems by Kolki   About universal well being, peace and love   *Absolutely Humane*

Betrayal

(Dedicated to a conscious compassionate sustainable civilized world)

[Who US/NATO forces are killing as suspected militants – Ancient <u>Hebrews</u>, <u>Buddhists</u>, <u>Early Christians</u>? <u>Kolki</u>]

When loggers' logging resemble <u>killing fields</u> -
Authorities in fisheries give license to kill <u>baby seals</u>!
Miners-Promoters destroy natural landscapes for quick profit!
Governments enact terrorism denying detainee's right to speak!
Judges silence defendants banning testimony from public -
Silence is consent equates to <u>betrayal</u>!

When occupying military kill pregnant women in labour!
Pre-emptive strikes destroy sleepy homes at peace afar!
Bulldozers level villages bewildering citizens in terror!
Tax money builds deadly weapons creating homeless and hunger!
Silence is consent equates to betrayal!

When governments terrorise people to join crusades!
Media spreads <u>Pandemic</u> rumours hiding <u>germ warfare secret</u>!
Military analysts justify <u>killings</u> as co-lateral damages!
Genetically modified seeds threaten pristine evolutionary process!
Silence is consent equates to betrayal!

When NATO forces kill civilians just speculating as militants!
UN sanctions punish countries with no record of aggression!
Defence Ministers <u>ban coverage</u> –
Of soldiers fallen in distant mission!
Governments <u>guard</u> terrorism <u>opposing</u> open public <u>investigation</u>!
Silence is consent equates to betrayal!

Poems by Kolki About universal well being, peace and love   *Absolutely Humane*

How Can We Help?
(Dedicated to a united conscious world – Written March 6, 2007)

Friends! How can we help? Is the biggest question!
After performing endless responsibilities in daily survival game!

As we work hand in hand as law abiding citizens!
Raising voice against militarism hurting national interest!
Remembering idle brains can be devils' workshops in secret –
Challenging source of intelligence from highly paid idle brains!
Or else, everything we achieve toward green and peace -
Be taken away from us by war after war at ease!

Personally, being more conscious embracing simpler means!
Ensuring household garbage free from plastics, glass and grease!
Composting everything organic except meat!
Recycling effectively wherever we live!
Cooking mostly at home healthy delicious meals!
Rewarding pets and children with fresh natural treats!
Minimizing wastewater from ponds, lakes and streams!
Avoiding synthetic fertilizer at home, garden and green!
Managing weeds to manage pests without pesticides and toxins!
Electing leaders who resonate with International treaties!

Making sure Green Party not making world less green!
Peace Corp not helping silently for (Armageddon) they dream!
Religion not preparing for Dooms Day blocking united prayers!
Non Governmental Organizations (NGO) not villains under cover!
Private media not too personal with gossips and commercials!
Newspapers deliver news with less shopping tips and coupons!
Pornography, abortions, not industries like drugs, soda and guns!

Thinking of the world as a nation full of beings and citizens!
From North to South, East to West, they are all God's Children!
Many evolved in, some inherited, the land of solar enchantment!
We must not let a few convert our living Heaven to Hell!

Recycling
(Dedicated to a pristine natural sustainable coexisting world)

We can keep our world clean very easily!
Following honest simple methodology!
Identifying the source of garbage - organic or technology!
And sharing responsibility accordingly!
Ensuring strict and fair accountability!
Advised by national recycling board of conscious recycling –
Where Members are elected –
From farmers, labourers, professionals and academics!

Organic garbage can go back to Earth without complexity!
Technical garbage must be controlled effectively -
Irrespective of private or government polluting entity!
Every home with a yard must make composting year round activity
Apartments/Townhomes/Condomoniums –
Make compost as community!

Water in and out of industry must be same quality!
Recycling trees the joint effort of paper, pulp and logging industry!
Chemical industry dissolves all pollutants from industrial chimney!
Oil industry takes responsibility for related products and spills!
Nuclear pollution must never come out of a nuclear facility!
Sewerage must be treated repeatedly ensuring safe releasability!
Airlines being the principal source of Global Warming -
Must ensure clean exhaust in high altitude global jet streams!
Military must own pollution and debris from all military activities!

The last but not least –
Recycling politicians who are for status quo mentality!
Analysts who feed on fear of negative economic activities!
Media that thrives on controversies!
Scientists who act as paid lobbyist of supremacist!

Super Power
(Dedicated to an united world)

Humans always strive to reach beyond limit!
Using physical strength, intent to compete!
Immense power hidden in the brain
Channelling through mind, body, voice and pen!

Every one has own idea about life!
About God, rituals, spirits, ethics and rights!
How community evolves with new goals insight!
Cities, villages, prosper sharing ideas for better life!
Civilizations emerge with achievements and pride!

Some strive for economic power!
Some for universal social welfare!
Some want to lead as religious leaders!
A few work hard to win ideological war
Converting country to military super power
Uniting imperialists as allied power
Using religion as political cover -
Only for supremacy as Super Power!

Poems by Kolki   About universal well being, peace and love   *Absolutely Humane*

Universal Super Power
(Dedicated to a united world void of fear and sufferings from Dominance and Supremacy)

[Israel was against the United Nations since inception occupying UN supervised Palestine; it got US/British Administrations to destroy it. Kolki]

As the divided parts of the Earth -
Became countries with borders!
Competition grew among each other -
Resulting in domination as Super Power!
Using resources and assets of lesser power!
Leading to military race with defensive posture!
Stockpiling weapons of mass destructions!
Requiring war to replenish new high tech weapons!
Destroying neighbourly trust of peaceful resolution!

But the problem can be an opportunity for final solution!
Enabling disarmament beyond doubts & fear of verification!
Making United Nations as the authority of mutual arbitration!
Where each country rules the world in periodic fashion!
Making it a sport for Super Power ambition!
With only goodwill and goodness toward world citizens in notion!
Reviving healthy competition for cooperative compassion!

Countries stay the same for government and infrastructure!
But the need to protect border disappear!
Trust among neighbours restore friendly atmosphere!
Conflicts get resolved in board rooms or amusement parks!
UN peace keeping forces become the only International Guard!

Qualifications for leaders are very straight forward!
Doesn't have to be lawyers, professors, doctors or engineers!
Profound knowledge of world history and culture -
A proven record of pre-emptive will to serve -
A competitive mind toward good will of care -
A proud soul for serving world better –
As the Universal Super Power!

Participatory Democracy
(Dedicated to true democratic world where people's voice rules without discrimination)
[**What good is expensive election where many don't vote and country is ruled my minority ideology!** – Kolki]

Let us recollect our memory!
The very definition of Democracy!
If three out of five agree –
Majority prevails without much controversy!

Now assume a fictitious country!
Of one million people with voting eligibility!
But only 60% cast votes with legitimacy!
And a party wins 55% of 60% of total ballot casting -
claiming majority!
That makes 33% people celebrating victory!
Often 20-25% of split votes ruling in reality!
Making decisions for the majority as undemocratic minority!
Giving in to the authoritative Intelligence and military!

Thus the due process in Multi-Party Democracy –
Divides people in the line of the party!
Encourages obedience to ideology as loyalty!
And the party stance takes priority over the country!
Often helplessly watching –
issues get hijacked from behind by pre-emptive military!
Strengthening corporate elites –
Against national and international integrities!

Now, imagine a world without any political party!
Citizens vote for candidates on issues good for the country!
No one is running a campaign with ideology!
Only with solutions and methodology for a better society!
On issues compiled by election agency -
As pre-election national survey –
For local and federal constituencies!

Participatory Democracy (Cont.)

Thus media won't hijack issues with diversions derogatory!
Private poll stars can't speculate anymore relentlessly!
Tax issues dealt by accountants and crime by Judiciary!
No place for political hypocrisy, just honesty and simplicity!
No need for endorsement, party line voting or lobbying!
Parliament not a mockery of partisan politics and infighting!
**No assassinations, physical or character –
ruining friends and family!**

It is simple like nation wide trivial examination!
Where ballots are not just a tick mark but evaluation!
Voters are markers –
Judging candidate's knowledge on issues and resolutions!!
For all municipal, provincial, and national general elections!

Election is fought over five most important issues!**
Making election a 2-day process as national holidays!
When media is absolutely committed for election coverage!
Ensuring voters have chances to view and hear the debates!
Making voting a mandatory participatory game!
Cities, Provinces or States –
Run primaries with issues as appropriate!
Five top scorers are selected for the general debate!
Then voters go to polls to mark candidates!
Top scorer wins based on issues weighted average –
Has option for joining provincial or central government!
2nd place will take the option not taken by the 1st place.

The top scorers who opted for the central government –
Would debate on five most important national and global interests!
All countrywide elected members would evaluate their speeches!
Again the top scorer is eligible as prime minister or president!
Runner up would be Deputy Prime minister or Vice President!
They will form cabinet –
With team members again based on weighted average!

Participatory Democracy (Cont.)

No elected member must be without a portfolio
Or a committee of associates!

Five top scorers from province or state –
Would debate on issues important for local-federal interface!
And all elected members would mark their scores on the debate!
Making the top scorer as the Governor or Premier,
The runner up as Lieutenant Governor or Deputy Premier!
Both will select cabinet –
from the members based on weighted average!

If every nation on Earth follows this principle
Irrespective of the size of the population
There will be no need for wars for competition!
No one will party –
While many suffering from destruction and starvation!
A world free from physical and character assassinations!
No pre-emptive strikes –
at the United Nation or distant mission!

A happy world live among neighbourly communion!
Recognizing partition inflicted geographic limitation!
Sharing each other's art, industry, science and religion!
Keeping <u>diplomacy</u> alive with honest and friendly discussion!
Enjoying the vastness of worldwide cultural evolution!
Watching civilization evolves without discrimination –
Solving issues progressively in peaceful union!

** - May vary as appropriate! This is a Draft which can evolve……

Poems by Kolki   About universal well being, peace and love   *Absolutely Humane*

Democratic Security
(Dedicated to open societies enlightened with truthful intelligence and judiciary)

[<u>Who</u> US administration protecting sealing <u>9/11 documents</u> and <u>wire tapping</u>? certainly NOT the <u>Americans</u>! <u>Who</u> <u>CSIS</u> and <u>RCMP</u> protecting <u>blocking</u> investigations and <u>blanking out</u> documents? Certainly NOT the <u>Canadians</u>! Kolki]

An <u>open Government</u> serves democracy the best!
Military intelligence must not enrich few in private!
All <u>findings</u> of judicial inquest must be in public safe!
Since judges tend to sympathize for holy crusades!
Whenever administration seal documents for ages -
Lawmakers <u>empower</u> commander with absolute strength -
They are running country as military commandment!

Flight recorders (<u>Voice-Data</u>) recovered from black boxes -
Must be analyzed <u>overtly</u> for resolving the <u>causes</u>!
Broadcasting Cockpit Voice tape instantly as recorded!
Never letting government documents be shredded –
Guarding felons hiding behind blanked out pages!
Not even in the name of God, religion, or Prophets -
Because hands on holy book often ignore holiness!

<u>Deaths and abuses</u> under protective cells -
Must be public investigations from the onset!
Lest <u>internal quest</u> delay and destroy evidence –
Breeding criminals inside authority in secret!

Otherwise, elected officials are just at the mercy -
Of 'imperial network' building Empire secretly!
Spending tax money lavishly, without accountability!
Building destructive kingdom against God's mercy!
Ruling as Emperor behind the vale of secrecy!
Making 'National Security' nightmares of citizens' insecurity!
As <u>protector</u> becomes the destroyer of <u>Democratic</u> Society!

Poems by Kolki   About universal well being, peace and love   *Absolutely Humane*

Intelligence
(Dedicated to an honest open neighbourly society)

[9/11 cover-ups and anomalies made CIA, FBI, US Military, suspected criminals why all confessions of detainees under their custody are assumed invalid! Kolki]

Our fight is with enemies who reside in virtual heaven!
What we do to save nations is absolute secret!
Tax payers must feed us billions without checks and balances!
We will rid the world from old weeds as evil suspects!
Our covert operations are prescriptions for democratic causes!

We cannot tell who when how and why -
But terrorists are working against us day and night!
Why threat level cycles in red orange yellow and red light!
Everyone must look around for suspects in disguise!
Back yard, front yard, under bed and hat,
wherever they may hide!

Senators cannot see our minutes its secret!
Congress can't view them its top secret!
Judiciary committee can't review its secretively secret!
Only officials who sympathise with our causes
Will praise our good work in media and speeches!
Glorifying the need to re-classify all declassified secrets!
Lest someone has idle-time to analyze our achievements!

Our mission is defined in Biblical events!
Our agents are licensed to kill for self defence!
Democratic laws for citizens work against our commitments!
We are intelligence - modern faith based guardian angels!

Poems by Kolki   About universal well being, peace and love   *Absolutely Humane*

American Orange Revolution
(Dedicated to true American spirit of freedom, peace and justice for all)

[When wise act ignorant, or indifferent, world becomes a dangerous place! Kolki]

My fellow Americans -
Must have learned form watching television
How quick orange revolution
Thrived around the parts of ancient civilization!

Okalahoma City Bombing and September 11 destruction
All related obstructions of justice sealing documentation
Detentions and abuses –
disregarding open honest investigation -
Made military, CIA, FBI, NSA, criminal organizations!
Requiring revival of American Orange Revolution!

It may seem unachievable -
But in fact could be very simple!
Without Politicians - who ignore truth as untouchables!
Ideologically bonded to 'The United Kingdom of Israel'!
Fear being labelled as 'soft on crime' and 'too liberal'!
Support troops violating international laws with arrogance!
Without Media - that avoid news as unmarketable!
And finally **without leaders** who whisper Armageddon!

Implementing pre-emptive peaceful mass revolution!
Guarding CIA, FBI, NSA, Pentagon, in Washington!
Releasing all documents for open distribution!
Taking over media like CNN for public television!
Converting FED as open government institution!
Ensuring media reflect population distribution!
And singing in chorus the song for American freedom -
"Then conquer we must, when our cause it is just,
And this be our motto: "In God is our trust."
And the star-spangled banner in triumph shall wave
O'er the land of the free and the home of the brave!".

American Orange Revolution (Cont.)

Finally, rejoicing with <u>American Pride</u> in friendliness!
Reassuring the world –
'The Statue of Liberty' was never meant for <u>military threats</u>!

Apology
(Dedicated to all who suffer in silence to maintain our way of life)

[I wonder where <u>Jesus</u> Loving Americans and Europeans are as worshipers of <u>Violent God</u> destroy <u>old world</u> for chaotic <u>new world order</u>! <u>Kolki</u>]

I apologized, sometimes in silence often aloud!
Every time an animal was abused or slaughtered!
A fellow human was tortured or murdered!
Military invaded foreign lands as destructive power!
Family homes demolished by missiles and bulldozers!

I apologized, before mowing lawns and trimming shrubs!
Being unable to help a pet scared looking for owner!
Unconsciously acting rude or unwelcoming to others!
Seeing people in need suffer cold Northern winter!
Whenever I forgot, thorns poked me as reminder!

I apologized for my indifference during daily chores–
Whenever elected officials appeared lying under oath!
Leaders justified missiles and troops bypassing votes!
Loggers got new license to cut more old growth!
Free trades forced citizens out of dear cozy homes!

I apologized –
When allied power used sanctions for military might!
A patient suffered uninsured in silence all night!
A child couldn't attend school in ghettos out of sight!
Dinner has been served but many starving nothing to bite!
Governments get hijacked by media, intelligence and elites!

If one needs reasons to apologize –
There are millions to maintain status quo of our way of life!

Santa Claus
(Dedicated to all who make a difference in day to day life on Earth)

If I were Santa Claus -
I wouldn't wait for the Christmas Eve
Hiding entire year in my North Pole factory
Watching children suffer, starve and die everywhere
From irresponsible distribution, inequity and war!
I would be out each day riding waves of light
To save and serve mostly the ones left behind!
Letting reindeer celebrate in the homey Arctic wild!

If I were Santa Claus -
I would be in the middle of every fight!
Waving flag and shouting 'HO HO HO' peace is insight!
Would be standing in courtroom watching trials
Helping lawyers for silenced victims behind prison wall!

If I were Santa Claus -
I would have gone to every house with a smile!
On chilled or warm Christmas night, dark or bright!
Knocking on the door detouring fireplace flight!
Asking children to thank their parent(s)
For year-round gift of <u>love</u>, guidance and cares!

If I were Santa Claus –
I would teach children – <u>truth</u> is the real <u>peace</u> foundation!
Halloween is 'all hallows eve' a holy occasion!
Departed souls not ugly as the masks of commercialization!
Body deforms decays and disappear as natural action!
But the soul wonders hallowed for eternal re-union!

If I were Santa Claus -
I would inspire people with goodness of <u>Saint Nicholas</u>!
Preaching <u>loving Gospels</u> of true <u>Jesus</u>!
That Kingdom of God is inside heart not in church!
Why United Kingdom of Israel –
is not <u>Vatican's Promise Land</u>'!

Santa Claus (Cont.)

That Christmas is not a time just for toys and bonus!
It's the time to sing <u>hymn</u> in chorus
Celebrating gift of life from Heavenly father and mother!

Got You
(Dedicated to universal bond and friendship)

A passenger was running to catch the train!
A fellow passenger gave a hand with a smile,
'I got you my friend'!

People were starving from drought and famine!
Fellow citizens arrived with food and water in time,
'We got you to save precious life divine'!

An electron was scared being shoot out of homey neutron!
Proton attracted it back home for new union!

Moon was wobbling separating from Earth!
Earth gave a hand recovering from sudden shock,
'I still got you in orbit locked'!

Earth was wondering through space homeless!
Sun gave a hand making it new friendly planet,
'I got you in right place to create limitless'!

Sun was traversing through galaxies frustrated!
<u>Milky Way</u> made it family much needed,
'I got you to emit light for ages'!

Galaxies where rushing in chaotic motion!
Our universe extended hand securing destination,
'I got you for endless evolution'!

Universes were running around feeling lonely aimless!
Until they became assured hearing,
'We got each other in a mesh'!

People were scared from death and abuse from war!
Peace mission arrived bringing hope in the middle of despair!
A dying soul was afraid of leaving the body so dear!
Until it heard a loving whisper, 'I got you, my dear'!

Thank you!
(Dedicated to all I know)

When my final moment comes
I may not be able to talk or shake hands!
Death may come from a sudden wound
Lonely at home or away in countryside beautiful!

So my friends, accept thanks in advance
As my gratitude for your love and care
Bringing in meanings to my earthly adventure
Sharing thoughtful time, warmth and shelter!

My heart wants to reward you all with gifts
Mind asks forgiveness for mistakes and misdeeds!
Soul prays for good health with family
Body wants to hug before saying good bye silently!

Please don't hide your emotion hearing my death!
If you want to party, go ahead and make my day!
If you cry, my path will be slippery for a while!
If you laugh, my journey will end fast!
If you curse, the trip will get a bumpy start!
If you feel sad, I will be glad I knew a soul attached!
If you miss me, I will feel the worth of my love!
If you scream, thunder will guide me to land of dream!

Please satisfy your heart without obligations!
I will be happy knowing someway I got your attention!

Death
(Dedicated to the family and friends of All Departed Souls)

Death –
Is the ultimate separation of a loved one!
No words, advice or consolation
Can compensate for the sudden loss;
Or heal the pain of the feeling of emptiness!
Only time and good reminiscences
Can help healing the pain of enlightenment!
As the soul reaches the new destination,
And realizes new dimension of consciousness.

Death is like changing clothes –
It's a journey to an unknown abode
Where the soul is finally free again
In the form of electromagnetic energy base
Traveling at the speed of light or above
As it gets ready for the next adventure!

We can only hope and wish -
That the departed soul gains enough energy
Realizing true love and acquiring true knowledge!
To go beyond the seventh layer of the ionosphere
Out in the vast and infinite universe,
To finally be in union -
With the very rhythm of creation!

About Kolki –

Born in Calcutta, India, October 17, 1954, son of a refugee parents from then East Bengal, now 'Bangladesh', leaving their Estate behind!

A converted Vegetarian who believes in non-violence and peace can be achieved throughout the world if the military powers are not worried about strategic interests at the cost of collateral damages which are real death and destructions.

Brought up in Southern Calcutta was always keen to know and learn about the people and their real condition even as a boy. A nature and animal lover, who maintained his faith in universal well being after graduating from Jadavpur University, Calcutta, in Electronics and Telecommunications Engineering and Computer Engineering, subsequently.

Lived and worked in Calcutta, Dayton - Ohio, Toronto - Ontario, Long Island - New York, Washington D.C.-Northern Virginia and San Francisco Bay Area. Obtained MBA Degree in Telecommunications Management, from Golden Gate University, San Francisco, during year 2000.

Pursuing Ph.D. at the University of Victoria, British Columbia, Canada, in the field of Applied Electromagnetics with a goal to perform fundamental research in Electromagnetic Waves and their effects on the environment considering living beings.

Also a singer who composed songs like 'Canadian Pride', 'Spirit of Victoria', 'Quest', 'Co-existence', 'Peace Now', 'Life is Simple' and 'New Year'! These songs are in the process of being album 'Absolutely Humane' since the songs reflect true universal values! Directed many Musical shows in North America and perform solo in community fund raising events.

About Kolki (Cont.) –

Wrote many peace related articles since 9/11, 2001, which can be accessed online via his poetry WEB Site www.kolki.com

Many poems by Kolki had been published in the International Society of Poets anthologies including 'Immortal Verses' and 'Secrets of the Soul', News Media and journals around the world, as well as part of Noble House collections like 'Colours of the Heart' and 'Theatre of the Mind', some winning awards!

Produced web site 'Kolkata (Calcutta) Beyond Mother Teresa' and working on future books 'Living with the lovebirds', 'Real path to 9/11', 'Universal consciousness' & 'Humane Cuisine'.

Also produced music CDs 'New Life', Tagore's Bengali Opera 'Shyama', 'Take Me To Your Heart' and 'Nostalgic'!

'Let us not waste any more time hunting for virtual terrorism! The whole world is hungry for peace and democracy achieved through mutual respect and understanding, not using bombs and missiles. War divides and destroys people and civilization, animal and environment, as the ultimate weapons of mass destruction'......Kolki.

Contact Address: 844 Royal Oak Ave, Victoria, BC V8X 3T2, Canada

ISBN 142512395-3